The Impossible is Possible

"Keep right on til the end of the road!"

Michael Hellawell

Michael Hellawell

The Impossible
Is Possible

A story of a Yorkshire lad

Dedicated to my beloved Brenda

I would like to thank the following for their invaluable help in getting my story onto paper.

Ronnie Preston
Julie Carson
Rob Grillo
Daniel Mosby

I would also like to thank the following for allowing us to use their photographs.

The Keighley News
Bradford Cricket League
doingthe92.com
A and B C Gum
Barrett candy cigarettes

CHAPTER 1
THE PINNACLE

As I stood in the tunnel in Belfast, I looked around and pinched myself. Here was the cream of English football, eleven players representing their country.

The names rolled off the tongue:
Ron Springett
Jimmy Armfield
Ray Wilson
Ron Flowers
Brian Labone
Bobby Moore
Jimmy Greaves
Alan Peacock
Freddie Hill
Mike O'Grady

And a certain Michael Stephen Hellawell playing at No.7, making up the numbers.

20th October 1962 would be engraved on my memory forever.

As I looked around it dawned on me that here was I, representing the best eleven players in England, There were no substitutes in those days. The capacity crowd roared and brought me out of my daydream, and I remembered where it all began. Nerves were soon replaced by expectations. Our opponents were Northern Ireland at Windsor Park, Belfast. They were led by the legend Danny Blanchflower and included wonderful players, Jimmy McIlroy, the darling of Burnley, and his teammate Alex Elder, Jimmy Nicholson and Sam McMillan of Manchester United and Billy Bingham of Everton, Terry Neil and Jimmy McGill from Arsenal and the Coventry duo Bill Humphries and Bert Barr, and in goal Bob Irvine. An impressive line-up indeed.

As I glanced across at Danny Blanchflower, my mind went back to being a young 17 year old lad, on my first day at Queens Park Rangers, still wet behind the ears and everywhere else for that matter. I was sent by my manager to Oxford Street in London to purchase a pair of new boots, Adidas boots, which were put on the bill of the account of QPR.

I sat down to try on the boots and there sat next to me was the captain of Tottenham Hotspur, none other than Danny Blanchflower, a "superstar" of the day. I was shocked and star-struck. He hadn't a clue who the ginger haired young lad was, but he put me at ease and told me I had made a good choice of boots and hoped I had a successful future. What a gentleman. And here I was playing against him (not with the same boots, I hasten to mention, and I had filled out a bit!).

I snapped out of my daydream very quickly as the capacity crowd roared us out onto the pitch.

More about the pitch later!

Sladen Street Today

CHAPTER 2
IN THE BEGINNING

Where have I seen those words written before?

30th June 1938.

The day I was born.

My parents, Alfred and Eileen, lived in Keighley and were both hardworking, typical Northern folk. Dad worked as a hospital porter and mum worked at Illingworth's, a ladies' outfitters.

I was born at St John's Hospital in Keighley, a small cottage hospital that had been converted from the old workhouse. It was a large, imposing Victorian building, built of stone with very small windows, so the previous occupants could neither look out nor "escape".

I was the first child to the couple, a bundle of joy, with a full head of bright red hair, a "ginger" or "carrot top" as we say in Yorkshire. It was a life changing moment for my parents, as with any new parents.

They brought me home to No. 12 Sladen Street; a small, typical terraced house of the time, two up, two down, with no bathroom or inside toilet, in fact no "mod cons" at all. A coal fire provided the warmth and a tin bath in front of the fire was as luxurious as you got.

As new parents, everything was trial and error, as with all new parents, but luckily for the couple, my grandparents,

Florence and George McCormack lived next door, together with Auntie Emily, so plenty of help was on hand if needed.

In those days, everybody helped each other and friends and neighbours mucked in as well. Nothing was thrown away – old rags and clothing were turned into rugs by cutting them up and pegging together. Home industry was a big saving on the price of shop bought goods, every penny counted.

Nobody locked their doors and people were in and out all the time. Everybody knew everybody else, where they lived, where they worked, who their children were etc.

No sooner had I celebrated my first Christmas than a certain Adolf Hitler was causing a stir in Germany, which would have repercussions for everybody in the civilised world. Just after my first birthday, the whole of Britain was stunned. Neville Chamberlain went to see Mr Hitler to talk some sense, but to no avail, the talks proving fruitless. Mr Hitler took no notice at all and Germany invaded Poland. On the 3rd September 1939, Mr Chamberlain the Prime Minister, broadcast on the radio that Great Britain had declared war on Germany and was coming to the aid of Poland and the free world.

Most people were just getting over the shock of another war. People were volunteering for the Armed Forces, but not enough, so conscription was brought in. Fighting men were needed by the country to take up arms against the enemy.

My father was called up and joined the Royal Air Force, leaving home for months at a time, leaving mum to look after the new baby, the house and everything else on her own. Luckily gran, grandad and Auntie Emily came to the fore.

Many people thought the war would be over very quickly and Adolf and co. would come to their senses once the British had entered the fray, but thoughts were the same in 1914 and the First World War was to drag on until 1918 (the "war to end all wars") **so it was a matter of "here we were again".**

Dad was away so much that he became a stranger to me, rarely coming home on leave and I was growing up fast without him. Luckily I was at an age when I knew nothing about grown up problems. Mum and her "team" kept me well fed and watered.

Memories of the war are a little vague, but I can remember the sirens going off and sheltering from the bombers. Keighley was lucky, if that is the correct term, that we missed the bombing as it was a small fry town. The Luftwaffe were after bigger fish in the form of cities, Bradford being just 12 miles away.

As I grew I remember the shortages and the queues. Everybody queued, for bread, for groceries, clothes etc. If you saw a queue, you joined it, just in case you missed out on something!

Everything was rationed, everybody got a ration book with coupons as well as a gas mask, in case the nasty Nazis dropped more than bombs – gas was a big threat.

If you really wanted something badly, you saved up your coupons, until you could afford it. (How would the youngsters of today manage eh?!)

All the neighbours really rallied round in these hard times, forming units and sharing food and clothes. Everybody mucked in. Never mind Mr Hitler, we are a tough lot in this country.

As small children, we were kept in the dark about the worldwide problems, all we wanted was food in our bellies and to play out in the fresh air. There were no TV's or Ipads and computers, you made your own entertainment - Hide and Seek, skipping, tig, British Bulldogs, hopscotch, which are all alien to the youngsters of today, who are lost without a screen to look at and a mobile phone glued to their hands. Sad to say it seems that the art of conversation is dying.

In 1947, the skipping and hopscotch took a back seat when the winter set in. Sledging was the game of the day when it started to snow, and snow and snow. I have never seen so much snow and the winter of 1947 was to become a record for the volume of snow falling.

The whole country was white, and the small villages around Keighley and into the Dales were cut off for weeks. Teams of men were employed to dig the villages out by hand. Once the snow had fallen, the sun shone for weeks. It was like a winter wonderland and the snow cutters all came home with wonderful suntans from the sun reflecting off the snow. Snow like that has not been seen since. My grandchildren have never seen snow. The communities just coped with 10 feet of snow all around, nowadays the country comes to a standstill if a sprinkle of snow comes down. The "Chelsea tractors" as they are called, the four wheel drive vehicles, come to a standstill as people abandon cars everywhere, and the trains stop for leaves on the line! We never missed a day at school, we just walked through the snow. Progress and technology now eh!

It seems that with all the modern technology, it's manpower that really counts. Today, with all the human rights and union dues, people are paid by their employers when they have days off, for sickness etc., so the modern workforce would rather stay in bed for the day than get out and work.

In our day, you went to school through hell or high water. We walked to school through snow three or four feet deep.

Kids today don't walk anywhere. If they can't get the car out, they have the day off. It wouldn't happen in my day. If you had time off, the "kid catcher" would be round asking your parents what was going on.

We got a bottle of milk at school, and in winter it would be frozen on the doorstep but would always be delivered. Same principles, work went on – if you didn't turn up you got no pay, so needs must – the principles that got the nation through the war.

CHAPTER 3
A TOUGH START

When I was two years old, yes two, I started school, at St Anne's Catholic School in the town.

St Anne's was run by a Catholic nun, Sister Gabriel. She was a very strict nun who believed in running things with an iron rod or hand. She dressed in a stiffly starched habit and frightened the living daylights out of the children.

Silence was the order of the day. "Children should be seen and not heard". If you crossed the line, a whack across the legs or a slap across the back of the head would soon have you back in line. Again, it was a different world from today, but this was 1940, a lifetime away.

After school, we couldn't wait to get out and play in the fresh air, and away from Sister Gabriel and the stinging legs. We would play in the streets and kids from the neighbouring streets would all come round. Football and cricket matches would take place with maybe twenty a side. We didn't play with balls, they were too expensive – we kicked anything, bully beef tins, old rags tied together. You had to be a rich kid to have a football and none of us were in that category.

The description of us was street urchins or ragamuffins, with hand me down clothes and clogs on our feet that sparked when we missed the tin and hit the cobbles on the street. All the kids mixed in, boys and girls and mums and grans all played together, until dark stopped the games or the sirens wailed. Then it was inside to listen to the radio or have a bath and bed.

Dad's visits were few and far between and I had to get used to him all over again when he came home. Mum and dad made the most of these visits and small celebrations were held before he returned to the RAF. Mum was pregnant and just before Christmas 1943, she gave birth to a baby boy, a brother for me, a new playmate and he was christened John. So Dad's leave had been fruitful, which meant mum now had two little ones to look after. Come in gran, grandad and aunty.

With Dad away I was now the man of the family, big brother and "boss" all at five years of age.

The war was on the turn and D-Day was fast approaching. Mr Chamberlain had been replaced by Winston Churchill as Prime Minister, morale was getting higher, and the USA had joined the fight again Hitler.

We listened to the radio every day for news and Mr Alvar Liddell and his distinctive voice kept everybody in the picture. There were no TV's in those days, we were not allowed to listen to William Joyce (or Lord Haw Haw as many knew him) he was a "bad man" as mum called him. When he said "Germany calling, Germany calling", the radio was soon switched off. He was later hanged as a traitor to the country. Violent days indeed.

Eventually the war turned full circle and Germany were overrun and were forced to surrender.

Parties were held everywhere. There were street parties and dancing in the street when Winston Churchill announced the end of the war. The grown-ups were on a high, but all us kids wanted to do was play cricket in the summer and football in the winter.

Everybody was grateful to be alive and unscathed. Dad eventually came home for good and I was no longer the man of the house and in charge of my brother, who was not quite two, and kicking everything that was loose, just like his big brother.

Rationing was still the order of the day, as food was still in short supply as were all "luxuries". The only luxury I had was going for a bath at the slipper baths on Highfield Lane, so I said goodbye to the tin bath in front of the fire.

I started a new school, St Anne's Catholic School in Keighley and my education started in earnest. I didn't much like the lessons and looked forward to the cricket and football after school. Cricket was my first love, but I was soon to realise the love of my life. Brenda was the one for me.

At church I became an altar boy, a big honour I thought, and my tasks involved getting the church ready for services. I had lots of tasks, helping the priest in everything he did, I used to fetch and carry and run errands. In some parishes they were known acolytes. I performed ceremonial duties for the priest, lighting the candles and carrying a lighted candle in procession to the altar.

On one such occasion, I was following the priest down the aisle when I suddenly felt very warm, very warm indeed!! Then panic set in when I realised I was on fire! People rushed forward and threw me to the floor, rolling me about, and soaking me in "holy water" to douse the flames. I thought hell and damnation was prevailing, but to relieved laughter, I was not hurt, just my pride. The service continued with the priest a little angry that the attention had been taken from him and people were laughing. A no-no in the Catholic Church at the time – laughter, whatever next!

In the same class as me in school was a certain Brenda Paton. We became good friends in a shy, bashful way. I would look across at her in the classroom and blush redder than my shock of ginger hair.

I was growing up fast and became a really fast runner (which would help in the future), but cricket came first, every lad in those days wanted to play for Yorkshire and I was no different. But Keighley was a rugby league town and the local team regularly got crowds of over 5000. Dad used to take me down to watch and it seemed like the whole of Keighley was in attendance, but rugby was a rough game, not for the likes of me, a stick thin lad with his heart set on cricket for Yorkshire.

On the home front, the war was a memory and mum and dad applied for a council grant for the construction of an inside toilet and bathroom for next door. Yes, an inside toilet, no more cold bums in winter. So now we were posh, no more trips to the slipper baths. I just "slipped" next door.

Things were looking up and at school, tests and exams were the order of the day. I was being educated as a good Catholic boy and both my parents and I were overjoyed when I passed my exam and I was accepted as a pupil of St Bede's Grammar School in Bradford. Dad bought me a cricket bat and took me to the county ground, Park Avenue, to watch the local derby versus Keighley.

St Bede's was another imposing Victorian building, but I had every opportunity to play cricket and football. The facilities were poor, the games were played on a gravel surface, but I never missed a chance to play for the school teams, both cricket and football.

The sports master thought I was too frail to play football and I was pushed out onto the wing (out of the way), so football took a back seat and I concentrated on cricket.

However, I must have shown promise out there as I was selected for Bradford Boys and then Yorkshire Boys Under 15 to play against Lancashire Boys at Boundary Park, the home of Oldham Athletic. The Lancashire boys were a good side with one standout player, a certain Wilfred McGuinness, who went on to play for England and of course Manchester United, until a bad injury forced an early retirement. In the future he was to become manager of Manchester United, following in the footsteps of Sir Matt Busby.

I was also selected to play cricket for Yorkshire Schoolboys again the old enemy Lancashire Schoolboys at the home of Yorkshire Cricket, Headingley, in Leeds. I scored an impressive 73 not out at Headingley, with all the Yorkshire hierarchy watching. I thought I had "made it" already!

Dad encouraged me in all I did. He followed every game I played – cricket, football – and when I received a write up in the local paper, he clipped out the passage made up a scrapbook. He kept everything, from scraps of paper to programmes. He was very supportive in my career, and I even found cuttings from the newspapers for my later career. He started me off on the right road. I think his only regret was that I didn't wear the "White Rose" for the Yorkshire first eleven.

He was a proud Yorkshireman and the pinnacle was to play for the County, never mind about England, in those days. From day one when he bought me a cricket bat, he thought I had it to play for our beloved Yorkshire. I think he was the proudest man in Keighley when I "made it" at Queens Park Rangers.

Dad was no different to any other dads around the county. He took cuttings form the newspapers whenever I was mentioned, whether in football or cricket.

After the games in those days, the papers were printed with the results. The local pinks or greens were printed near the grounds so the fans could get the results as soon as possible. Every town had their own local paper and it was a competition to get the results printed, **so** the fans could have them as they walked out of the grounds. The football results were big business, Littlewoods or Vernon's ran football pools to get the fans interested and they would make lots of people rich. The Lottery has taken over but I think you can still do "the pools".

St Anne's School

St Anne's church (right)

St

Bede's School

CHAPTER 4
THE START, JULY 1955

One night I was sat at home with my parents when a knock came to the door. My father answered it and there stood in front of him was a smartly dressed, middle aged man. He introduced himself as a Mr Saunders, a school teacher from Leeds who was also the northern scout for the London football club, Queens Park Rangers.

At that time Queens Park Rangers were playing in the 3rd Division South, not exactly the Premiership of nowadays, but money was tight, rationing had just finished and the leagues in the lower halves were split North and South to save money. As fuel was still scarce, travelling long distances was discouraged.

Mr Saunders had seen me playing for Salts Football Club and asked my parents if they would let me travel to London to seek my fame and fortune. My mind was racing, not thinking of the money I would receive, but the three months I would get off in the summer to play cricket. Lots of players at the time played football in the winter and cricket in the summer. Arthur Milton of Bristol City and Gloucestershire and of course Denis Compton of Arsenal and Middlesex, who both played for England.

My father had no doubts about my ability, and that I could "make it", but London was a world away from the Yorkshire Moors and he asked the Scout for time to think about it. The Scout agreed to return in a week's time.

During the week that followed, my father suggested that he would go to Huddersfield Town, where I had played a few games for their youth teams. His thinking was Huddersfield was a local club and I could stay at home. When my dad spoke to Huddersfield, they said they were not interested as I was too frail and wouldn't make it as a professional, so those hopes were dashed, but I still had the offer to fall back on.

Mr Saunders arrived back as promised and I signed the forms to make me a professional footballer for Queens Park Rangers.

I was told to go to London to their Loftus Road ground and report to the manager Mr Jack Taylor. My heart was beating out of my chest as I said goodbye to my parents at Keighley Railway Station to make my way to the capital, a seventeen year old boy.

The train to Leeds steamed into the station and I climbed aboard in a complete trance, but looking forward to the great adventure to come. Leeds station was a throb of people running every which way, everybody seemed to know where they were going, nobody noticing the lanky red-haired lad going to the "smoke" to make his fortune as a professional, yes a professional footballer. There was not long to wait until the express to London pulled in at the platform and I boarded with a million thoughts zooming round my head. What will it be like? What if I got lost? Will I get on with the other players? What will the manager say to me? My mind was racing faster than the steam train.

I didn't realise we had started moving and already Wakefield and Doncaster had sped by. I was out of Yorkshire and on my way.

We passed Highbury, the home of Arsenal and pulled into Kings Cross. My mind was clearing now as I had to get to Shepherd's Bush, the home of QPR. I had never been to the

Big City before and everybody seemed to know where they were going, except me.

I had all the directions written down and took five minutes to study the Underground as all the Londoners went about their business in what seemed a rush. The "tube" was also new to me and I was nervous and stood all the way as I didn't want to miss a stop. I was going "up west" as they say in London, the posh part, Hammersmith and Fulham. I found Loftus Road and reported to Mr Jack Taylor. We had a brief chat and he informed me I was their youngest recruit, which put me back a bit, but before I had time to think, he had sorted digs out about 200 yards from the ground and told me to go back to Oxford Street to a sports shop and purchase a new pair of boots and charge them to QPR.

So back on the tube and into the heart of the City. I found the shop and introduced myself to the assistant who brought me a pair of Adidas boots, brand new, shiny black with the famous three white stripes, standing out like a sergeant's stripes. As I tried them on, the guy sitting next to me, also trying boots on, said "Good choice" and I looked up and there was the legend Danny Blanchflower, the captain of Tottenham Hotspur and Northern Ireland!

What an introduction to London, roads are paved in gold and new boots and superstars talking to me, a scrawny lad from Yorkshire. Could it get any better? I felt ten feet tall!

The accommodation QPR had arranged for me was a terraced house on Thorpebank Road, just walking distance from Loftus Road. Other QPR players were there and I was made welcome by a young goalkeeper, Ro Springett (who made a name for himself at QPR, Sheffield Wednesday and England). Ron was a local lad from Fulham so knew his way about. He showed me the ropes and pointed me in the right direction.

The next day I reported for my first training session. Pre-session training was very hard and I wasn't as fit as I thought, but being the youngest on the books, youth pulled me through against the more experienced players. Training was running, running and more running, day after day. The season was fast approaching and time was not on our side. Playing for Queens Park Rangers was becoming a reality.

My first game for QPR was in the second team who played in the Football Combination. The reserves played on small ground around London, not much travelling, on Saturdays but on Wednesdays the third team played at the big grounds around London, Highbury, the home of Arsenal; White Hart Lane, the home of Tottenham Hotspur; Stamford Bridge, the home of Chelsea, as well as Upton Park and Charlton's ground, The Valley.

It was fabulous to play at all these grounds, even though they were empty. I was told to stay on the wing at all costs, and beat the full back with my pace, "hug the touchline" was etched into my mind. In those days, the only grass to be found was on the wing, just mud down the middle. My new Adidas boots were brilliant on the grassy surfaces.

I played in the second team from August to February and I was getting fitter and fitter and faster and faster. "As fit as a butcher's dog" as we say in Yorkshire. On the field I was doing fine and getting used to life in the Big City. I was settled in my digs, I had found a lovely church to worship in, being a good Catholic boys and things were looking rosy.

On the 9 February 1956, I was summoned to the manager's office and he informed me that he was selecting me for the first team at the weekend. I was a nervous wreck until the Saturday and I made my first team debut on 11 February 1956, against Exeter City, so now I really was a professional footballer, earning all of £7 per week, yes you read right £7 in winter and £6 in summer.

The game was just a blur and I don't remember much, probably a mixture of nerves and excitement. I was up against a left back called Alf Sherwood, a Welsh international, but I was a raw, quick 17 year old, who was told to stick to the wing and skin him with my pace.

The game was broadcast on the radio (no "Match of the Day" then). My proud parents had travelled down from Yorkshire to see my debut. The QPR fans were magnificent to me all game and made me feel so welcome, which calmed my nerves. The game was a dull affair, ending in a 0-0 stalemate. Most of the team were so disappointed not to have won the game and I was probably the only one with a smile on my face, which remained there for days after.

The grin wasn't to last as this was to be my first and last first team game that season. It was a learning curve, my manager said, which seems to be the stock answer even to this day.

The season ended in April and I couldn't wait to get back to Yorkshire, to see Brenda and don my whites and get back to the game I really loved, cricket, a religion in Yorkshire at that time.

GETTING READY FOR THE START

MICHAEL HELLAWELL, 17-year-old Keighley winger, who has signed for Queen's Park Rangers FC, photo-graphed in training at his new club's ground yesterday. Hellawell once a Salts football

CHAPTER 5
CRICKET LOVELY CRICKET

Back home in Keighley, I went down the nets to get some valuable practice. Playing for Keighley in the Bradford League, I hoped would be the stepping stone to the next step up, Headingley and the Yorkshire team.

It was great to practice every day and after some good performances for Keighley, I was invited to attend the nets at Headingley, the headquarters of Yorkshire County Cricket Club - the Holy Grail! When I arrived I found I had to make a huge step and get to another level to make a County cricketer.

The two coaches taking the nets were Arthur Mitchell and Maurice Leyland. Maurice Leyland had been a Yorkshire regular for 26 years, scoring 1000 runs in a season, and seventeen seasons on the trot and played in 41 test matches for England and Arthur nicknamed "ticker" played in 6 tests and scored over 20,000 first class runs, true legends. I thought I was a good all-rounder and these two pushed me to the limit.

Trying to get in the Yorkshire team at that time was harder than winning the lottery. The 50's and 60's were the golden era, especially in Yorkshire. The names trip off the tongue:-

Illingworth; Close; Trueman; Appleyard; Sutcliffe; Binks; Stott; Taylor; Padgett; Bolus; Sharpe; Wilson; Ryan; Hampshire; Boycott; Nicholson; Hutton etc. etc, to name just a few. Pick a team from that lot and they would beat anybody and here was a young lad having a try, an uphill task, but keeping going.

"Don't give up" was my motto.

So back to London to make my living and pre-season training for the new season, 1956-57.

We started hard and it got a lot harder, running miles, up and down the terracing, counting the steps to the top of the stand and back down. We hardly ever saw a ball, the coaches had it in their minds that if we didn't see a ball during the week, we would want it and look after it on a match day.

In August 1956, the manager called me into his office. I racked my brain to think what I had done wrong, but when I got there, he told me to sit down. He then told me he was going to put me in the first team for an indefinite period. I was shocked and elated, an honour for an 18 year old. I managed to keep my place all season and showed "prowess" as my manager put it. But as any young lad, I had great games, good games and sometimes poor games, but the manager was true to his word and stuck with me. The fans had no doubts and it was great hear my name chanted from the stands. Being on the wing, you hear most of their comments!

CHAPTER 6
IN THE ARMY NOW

My world came crashing down in February 1957. Britain was still in war prevention mood and conscription was still on the statute books for all 18 year old men. I received my call up papers for my National Service for two years of my life for my country.
I was to report to Crookham in Hampshire, a large army base, and I was to join the Royal Army Medical Corps on 4th April.

The 4th April 1957 duly arrived and I reported for duty to start six weeks of basic training at Queen Elizabeth Barracks which comprised of a lot of wooden hugs housing 2500 men. So Private Michael Stephen Hellawell 2334815 was now a "soldier" in her Majesty's Army and one of thousands of men doing their duty for Queen and Country.

The bugle called at 5am every morning and duty called. The sergeant major would bark and we all jumped. His voice could strip the paint off the wall. Six weeks of basic, arduous training had begun. Luckily I was very fit from my football training, but lots of the other lads would struggle.

Our days were spent marching, marching and more marching, and if weren't marching, we were cleaning kit. (The only time I have cleaned anything in my life, according to Brenda!).

The parade ground was my second home and my kit was as shiny as a new pin. The Sergeant Major would soon come down on you like a ton of bricks if it wasn't perfect. Sleeping in dormitories together and working in teams was designed to make us into a fit unit to save the Queen.

The six weeks passed very quickly and we were all apprehensive as to what was coming next, where we would be posted etc. We were all fitter than ever and ready for anything.

I was summoned into the office of Major Howells. Marching in with the Sergeant Major, I stood to attention and saluted.

"Hellawell 2334815."
"SIR!!"
"Stand easy Hellawell." replied the Major.
"I hear you play cricket as well as being a professional footballer."
"Yes Sir!"
He then told me he had plans for me. "We are going to keep you here at this base and you can play cricket and football for the camp teams."

That sounded brilliant, just the ticket, playing sport whilst training to be a medic. Not bad eh?

I was to get an even bigger surprise not long after. Major Howells once again summoned me to his office. I stood to attention.

"Hellawell 2334815."
"Sir."
"At ease Hellawell."
"Now then Hellawell, a Mr Arthur Turner has asked if he can come and see you at the camp and I have given him permission," said the Major in a relaxed non-Army tone.

Arthur Turner was the manager of League Division One side Birmingham City and famous for being the amateur player for Charlton Athletic in the 1946 FA Cup Final, before he had even played a league game because of the War. The league was suspended during the War years. He wanted to know if I would sign for Birmingham City.

City were one of the leading teams in the country, a big city team, who had reached the FA Cup final in 1956, only to be beaten by Manchester City. The 1956 final was to become known as the "Revie final", after the Manchester City centre forward, Don Revie.

In those days, every player stuck to their positions; the right winger stayed on the right, the left winger the left, full backs stayed at the back, the centre half stuck down the middle etc. etc. But Revie broke all traditions as a centre forward and instead of sticking down the middle, he wandered all over, confusing the Birmingham defenders, who didn't know how to counter those moves, and Manchester City won 3-1 in the battle of the big city teams.

I couldn't believe that a First Division side wanted to sign me. The nerves and excitement were playing on my mind until the following Tuesday when Mr Turner was to arrive. Tuesday duly arrived and I was a bag of nerves. Summoned to the Major's office to be introduced to Mr Turner, I was told to sit down. I think I might have fallen down, I was that nervous!

Mr Turner sold the club to me and told me that he had been in touch with Queen's Park Rangers with a proposal to sign me, and that QPR had accepted an offer of £6,000 plus a player to go to QPR, Bill Finney, for my signature. He then outlined the way he wanted Birmingham to play and I would fit in with his plans perfectly. He outlined the salary I would get, the starting pay was to be £12 per week and £7 appearance money every game I played, whilst still doing my

National Service. This was a huge rise from my £7 per week at QPR.

Not much thought was needed! To play in the First Division and money to match, I signed on the spot. There were no agents in those days. I just couldn't believe my good luck. My future looked bright. I was going to play for one of the biggest clubs in the land in the First Division of the Football League. All I needed to do now was see out my National Service.

Major Howell was brilliant and he got me a job on the camp as a medical clerk in the office and he made sure I played cricket and football for the camp teams.

The camp football team was a really good side with other lads in the team who were also doing their National Service. With Alex Nichol from Hibernian in Scotland, Sid Russell of Brentford and George O'Brien from Leeds United, we were usually too strong for the other units in the Army.

I was selected to represent the British Army at a game in Poole, Dorset and one of my team mates was a certain Gerry Hitchins. Gerry was to make his name with various clubs – Cardiff City and Aston Villa. He caused a stir in 1961 among the football community by rejecting English Football who had a maximum wage ruling for all players of £20 per week (yes £20) and he went to ply his trade in Italy with Torino and Inter Milan. Gerry was a classy centre forward with an eye for goal.

The time in the Army flew past and I was soon to be de-mobbed. The 1957-58 season had just started and in early September I was called into the office by Major Howell. You know the drill by now! Major Howell informed me that he had had a request from Birmingham City. They had selected me to play and make my debut against Newcastle United at

St. Andrew's in Birmingham. Major Howell had given his permission and I was to travel to Birmingham on Friday to book into a hotel close to the ground, where Birmingham had reserved a room for the night. The game was to kick off on Saturday 7th September 1957, 3.00pm. All games kicked off at 3.00pm Saturday, a tradition that only TV would break in the future.

Newcastle United at that time were struggling a bit. Jackie Milburn had just left the club, but they had some great players in Bobby Mitchell, Bob Stokoe, George Eastham and Jimmy Scoular, all household names.

Jackie Milburn ("wor Jackie") now has a statue outside St James' Park. Jimmy Scoular, the Scottish international played 247 games for United. Jimmy Hill (not the one with the chin) was a Northern Ireland international. Bob Stokoe, played for Newcastle 261 times and became even more famous when he managed arch rivals Sunderland to an FA Cup Final victory in 1973 against the overwhelming favourites Leeds United. Bob has a statue outside the impressive Stadium of Light in Sunderland. Bobby Mitchell, the Scottish International who played 367 times for United. Lastly George Eastham, who went on to play for Arsenal, became famous   for a 1963 court case which was a landmark for the professional game, improving players wages and getting free movement for players.

CHAPTER 7
DEBUT FOR CITY

With Major Howell's permission, I boarded the train to Birmingham and arrived in the afternoon, finding my hotel near the ground. After a restless night, tossing and turning, nerves and adrenalin were kicking in. I couldn't wait to get to the ground, pacing and up and down in the hotel bedroom.

Eventually I couldn't wait any longer. A lanky nineteen year old, ginger-haired boy with energy to spare, I nearly sprinted to the ground. I was let in by the doorman and I went straight to the dressing room, not knowing what to expect, not having been to Birmingham or met the players, having had no training with them or conversation.

In the dressing room, the shirts were hung on pegs in numerical order, so I say down next to my number 7, the only one there. I had arrived a good hour and a half before kick-off, raring to go, bouncing with anticipation and lots of nervous energy.

The other players came in in dribs and drabs, seasoned professionals, just another day to them probably. There was Gil Merrick, the goalkeeper, Jeff Hall, the English International, Eddie Brown. Some I knew, others I didn't. They all looked at this kid sat there waiting and all said "hello" and chatted like old friends. My nerves were settling a bit now as we all got changed.

The manager arrived and had a few words, told us to play our natural way. I was told to stick out on the wing. No tactics, no team talk, just a "get out there and do the business"!

St Andrews
Birmingham
7th September 1957

Birmingham City   v   Newcastle United

1. Gil Merrick	1. Ronnie Simpson
2. Jeff Hall	2. Alf McMichael
3. Ken Brown	3. Ron Batty
4. Lew Boyd	4. Bob Stokoe
5. Trevor Smith	5. Tom Casey
6. Roy Warhurst	6. Jimmy Scoular
7. Mike Hellawell	7. Bobby Mitchell
8. Noel Kinsey	8. Bill Curry
9. Eddie Brown	9. Reg Davis
10. Peter Murray	10. George Eastham
11. Alex Govern	11. Jimmy Hill

Birmingham City 1 – Newcastle United 4

Mike Hellawell 1   Bill Curry 2
                                    Bobby Mitchell 1
                                    Jimmy Hill 1

Crowd 29,784

Gil Merrick was an England International goalkeeper who was to play 485 games for City and 23 times for England. He became manager later and a stand is named after him at St Andrews.

Jeff Hall played 227 times for City and 17 times for England. Jeff tragically died of polio at the age of 29. Polio was widespread in the country at that time and vaccinations were proving unpopular. After Jeff's death, his widow went on TV to plea and immunisation rocketed around Britain and polio is now a controlled disease.

Eddie Brown was a tough centre forward who played 158 times for City. The list is endless, all seasoned professionals:-

Ken Green	401 games
Len Boyd	255
Trevor Smith	365 and 2 England Caps
Roy Warhurst	213
Noel Kinsey	149 and 7 Welsh Caps
Peter Murphy (Spud)	245 165
Alex Govern	

And here was a young Keighley lad trying to impress.

I felt way out of my depth amongst these players and a little "star struck" but Gil and Jeff soon put me at my ease and told me just to enjoy the game. We went out onto the pitch five minutes before kick-off, had a five minute kick about and then the game started.

When play started I was not the only one out of my depth. The entire Birmingham team were thoroughly outplayed by a slick Newcastle United team who were knocking the ball about, making us all look like boys against men. We lost the game 4-1 and it could have been much worse.

The highlight of the game, for me at least, was when I was going down the wing as ordered. I cut inside the full back and hit a shot with my left foot and scored on my debut. There was not much celebrating, I just thrust my arms into the air, and the crowd were going wild, no sliding on my knees into the corner like the modern players. How my knees ache when I see that nowadays. I wish I could tell you it was a screamer from 30 yards but in fact my left foot (as Gordon Banks was to say later) was for standing on. The ball bobbled into the corner in which seemed like slow motion. At least me and the 30,000 crowd had at least something to shout about.

We trooped off the field at the end, well and truly beaten. It was to be my first, and last, appearance of that season and I went back to the Army camp to complete my National Service.

Jeff Hall

CHAPTER 8
TRAGEDY FOR FOOTBALL

Back in camp, tasks were mundane. There was plenty of paperwork to do, endless red tape, **not** much medical training, but I knuckled down to complete my two years. Days rolled into each other, one day being the same as the last. Up at five, kit spotless for inspection, endless paperwork, but two years was not a lifetime. However, one day in 1958, on the 6th February, an event happened that was to affect me, football, and the whole nation.

I was listening to the radio when the programme was interrupted by a newsflash, which sent shivers down my spine. An aeroplane had crashed in the snow in Munich, Germany. The plane was carrying the players and officials of Manchester United, a charter flight returning from a European Cup game against Red Star, Belgrade. The plane had stopped to refuel in Munich and crashed on its third attempt to take off in a heavy snow storm.

Over the next hours, more news came out. Everybody was glued to the radio for news. The full horror came out in the following bulletins. Twenty three people had lost their lives in the crash, including crew, reporters who were following the team and eight players from the Manchester United first team.

The players who perished were

Eddie Coleman, aged 21
Liam Whelan, aged 22
David Pegg, aged 22
Mark Jones, aged 24
Geoff Bent, aged 25
Tommy Taylor, aged 26

Roger Byrne, Captain, aged 28

Other players were injured and fighting for their lives in hospital, including Duncan Edwards, Bobby Charlton and the manager Matt Busby.

These were the "Busby Babes" who were playing in Europe as one of the first English teams to play the European competition, and had only stopped in Germany to refuel.

Other players were injured and some like Harry Gregg, the Irish goalkeeper, were to become heroes, going back into the wreckage to help others.

Duncan Edwards was arguably the best player in English football, a colossus of a man who could play in any position and would have had a great future in the game, but he succumbed to serious head injuries some fifteen days after the crash, becoming the eighth member of the team to die. Bobby Charlton was to recover and become a national icon, Sir Bobby, who was to win every honour in the game, including the World Cup in 1966.

The crash decimated the United team and had an effect on the whole country, and was one of those moments when you remember where you were when you heard the news. Football and the whole world mourned the loss of those young men, and now Manchester United are one of the biggest clubs in the world.

vgMatt Busby recovered from his injuries in time to see his young team get to the Cup Final in May, but the fairy-tale ending was not to be, with United beaten by Bolton Wanderers in the final, everybody outside Bolton cheering on United.

Summer came round with everybody still stunned, but army life just went on like clockwork.

CHAPTER 9
BACK TO THE OLD ROUTINE

The Army was used to traumas and tragedies and life went on, the parade ground, the kit, the paperwork. The cricket season had started and I was asked to play for the camp against a local club side. The captain asked if I would field in the slips, no problem, as I stood next to the wicket keeper. He said to me that we had better go back a few yards and eventually we were over 20 yards back behind the wicket.

I thought to myself "Blimey, who have they got bowling, Fred Truman?" It turned out the young lad opening the bowling was Ken Higgs, who was playing minor county cricket for Staffordshire at the time. He went on to have a magnificent career opening the bowling at Lancashire with Brian Stathum playing 511 first class matches, taking 1,600 wickets and making 15 test appearances for England. The keeper was correct, with the ball flying through at chest height.

Finally my two years of National Service were up and I was demobbed from the Army on 1 April 1959. Two years older and wiser, I knew paperwork and cleaning and a small bit of medical work, plus I was very fit from all that square bashing.

So it was back to Birmingham for the last month of the Season.

I was met by a city in mourning due to the death of Jeff Hall. All the City players were tested for polio as in those days after games, all the players jumped into a large bath together to wash. Thanks to Mrs Hall, vaccination queues were all over the city.

Things gradually got back to normal at the club, but the manager who had signed me, Arthur Turner, had left and a new manager had arrived, Pat Beasley, who had played 406 league games and played for England in 1939. Mr Beasley didn't rate me much as a player and he put me in the third team in the Birmingham League for the last few games of the season.

The summer break couldn't come quick enough and I returned home to Keighley, playing cricket for my home town club, and catching up with Brenda, who I was courting now.

JEFF HALL

On 23rd November 2019, I was invited to attend the unveiling of a Blue Plaque in memory of Jeff Hall, in the village of Wilsden, close to where I live, some sixty years after his untimely death.

The village of Wilsden, where Jeff lived and was brought up, came out in force to honour Jeff, their local hero.

A representative of Birmingham City travelled up and made a short speech before Jeff's nephew Chris Miller performed the ceremony, unveiling the plaque which was made available by Wilsden Parish Council.

It was good to see a good turnout by the locals, especially many youngsters turning out in their football shirts of their favourites, and they all seemed in awe of Jeff's shirts from Birmingham City and England together with his England Cap, which were on display.

Jeff is buried in the local cemetery in Shay Lane, Wilsden, with his grave being given a makeover with funds from the ex-players association of Birmingham City.

Gone but not forgotten.

CHAPTER 10
THE REAL START AT CITY

Not knowing what to expect I returned to Birmingham for the start of the 1959-60 season, and was met by a stern Mr Beasley. Pre-season was the usual running and running and sweat pouring from every opening. I was still physically fit from the Army but not fit enough to be in Mr Beasley's plans. After the first team made a very poor start to the season, Mr Beasley was sacked and Gil Merrick was put in charge.

Gil must have seen something in me that Mr Beasley hadn't and he put me straight back in the first team and I was to play on the right wing. I took the place of Harry Hooper, who was a crowd favourite, and had played 105 games. Harry was sold to Sunderland.

Gil instructed me to stay out on the wing and beat my opponent with my electric pace. Not many fullbacks were as fast as me in those days, but could hit you hard if they did catch you.

I thrived out on the wing and became a first team regular, staying in the first team all season and I was getting fitter and faster with full time training. The future looked bright, I was a first team regular in the First Division and I was about to get married to my childhood sweetheart, Brenda, whom I had known all my life, playing in the streets and going to the same school and in the same class. We were best pals and romance blossomed from a very early age. We did everything together, we were avid walkers in the countryside of Yorkshire "walking out together", as they said at the time, and we were regular cinema goers.

Brenda was a big fan of the musicals, such as "Singing in the Rain" with Gene Kelly. But her favourite, Bristol born Hollywood Star was Cary Grant (I can't think why!), who was making films with Alfred

Hitchcock, for example, "Rear window" and "North by Northwest". The Hollywood stars packed out the cinemas in Keighley and the whole country, the golden age of cinema.

Myself and Brenda had the same interests in life. Christianity mattered to us both and we worshipped together whenever we could. Although my job and Army service kept us apart at times, we always stayed in touch with regular letters criss-crossing the country. The postman would have sore feet, trudging to Brenda's house.

When back in Keighley, my first port of call was always Brenda's house for a reunion and catch up, under the watchful eye of her father, who kept a close eye on her, as all fathers did at the time. If Brenda went to a dance, her father would always be there at the close to see her home safely. Brenda loved dancing and when I was home, we would go to the dance halls for a good time. I say *we* danced, I just turned up. As I have said earlier, and Gordon Banks reiterated, my left foot was for standing on and had a mind of its own, the right foot was the order of the day. I didn't much like dancing but as long as I was with Brenda, the world was a better place.

So our schooldays became adult days and I plucked up the courage to ask her to marry me. She said "yes" – yippee! Asking her father was more nerve wracking, worse than playing in front of 40,000 people, but tradition even to this day.

We had to get married in the close season and we arranged to be married on 8th July 1960 at St Anne's Church, Keighley. My best man was Robin Stubbs, the centre forward. Surrounded by friends and family, we were now Mr and Mrs Hellawell and we had a reception at the Albert Hotel in the town, and set off for a short honeymoon in Scarborough (or Scarbados as the locals call it), a beautiful seaside resort on the East Yorkshire coast.

The Albert Hotel

The honeymoon long gone, it was back to Birmingham for the 1960-61 season and now being a "season pro" and a married man, I needed suitable accommodation for myself and my new bride. The club offered me a house to rent on the outskirts of Birmingham, a small suburban area called Sheldon, close to the city, a similar size to Keighley. We soon settled in and pre-season started.

Brenda got herself a job at BUPA, next door to the oratory, a small Catholic chapel run by the priests, one of whom was John Henry Newman, who has just been canonised by the current Pope Francis.

New signings had been made by the club in the close season, one of which was Jimmy Bloomfield from Arsenal, an inside right. We soon developed a good partnership on and off the pitch.

Jimmy was London lad who had played 210 times for Arsenal and stayed at Birmingham for 4 years, playing 123 times and playing at Under 25 level. Jimmy was an excellent passer of the ball, full of running. He was to become a manager after his playing days, including managing a Leicester City side in the 70's that fans still talk about to this day one of the great Leicester City teams. His untimely death at the age of 49 shocked the football world.

Gil also brought in a Spanish coach Emilio Aldecoa. He was a former Spanish International and was the first Spaniard to play in the Football League, the first of many.

The season itself was an up and down affair. Highs included beating the likes of Arsenal, Chelsea, Manchester United and Manchester City. But lows, crushing defeats at Wolves 5-1, Tottenham Hotspur 6-0, but worst of all a 6-2 mauling at the hands of our local and fiercest rivals, Aston Villa.

We finished 19th in the League, just two places above the dreaded drop and an average/poor season was compounded by the fact I was joint top scorer with just 10 goals.

The FA Cup was a bit brighter and we progressed to the fifth round. In the third round, we played Nottingham Forest away and managed a 2-0 win, then in the fourth round, it was Rotherham United at home and we had a thumping 4-0 win. We were then drawn at home to Leicester City where we could only manage a 1-1 draw in front of a huge crowd of 53,589. In the replay at Filbert Street, we lost 2-1.

The League Cup was not much better. We were drawn against Bradford Park Avenue away, a ground I knew very well, having played cricket there. Bramall Lane and Park Avenue were used as county grounds by Yorkshire as well as for the football. The game was a tight game played in front of a crowd of baying Yorkshiremen. I managed to score and we won 1-0, much to the annoyance of 4,736 Yorkshiremen. Next round was home to Plymouth Athletic and a drab 0-0 draw (a dulux game as a friend puts it) like watching paint dry. In the replay we were soundly beaten 3-1.

CHAPTER 11
INTER CITIES FAIRS CUP

The previous year, Birmingham City, one of the first English clubs to enter the European competition, had been beaten in the final by Barcelona and had qualified for this year's competition by reaching the final.

In the first round, first leg, we were drawn to play the Hungarian side Ujpest Dozsa, on the 19th October. At home, under the floodlights at St Andrew's, the atmosphere was electric, and European opposition brought out the best in the fans. We didn't play well but scraped a 3-2 win, and as they say, a win is a win. It gave us a one goal lead to take into the second leg in the beautiful Hungarian capital city of Budapest, on the banks of the river Danube.

We arrived in Hungary on the 25th and had a quick look round the city, half of which is on one side of the Danube, Buda and the other side of the city is well worth a visit with its historic buildings and friendly people. But we had no time for sightseeing, we were here to complete a job.

We completed the operation on the 26th October with a professional 2-1 win, taking the tie 5-3 on aggregate.

In the next round, we were drawn again the Danish side K B Copenhagen and the first leg was to be played at their tiny ground in the Danish capital on 23rd November. On a small pitch in a tiny stadium, in front of a packed 2,500 (wonderful, wonderful Copenhagen) fans, we came away with a 4-4 draw. Every shot seemed to be goal, but at least we were level to take home with us. On 7th December, we were hosts for the second leg at St Andrew's.

On the much bigger playing surface at St Andrew's, the Danes were out of their depth and seemed to be overawed by the occasion, and we ran out easy winners 5-0 with yours truly managing to get on the score sheet, 23,000 blues fans went home very happy that night!

So now we were in the semi-final which wasn't to be played until April the following year, 1961. The draw was made and we were pulled out of the hat to play one of Italy's most famous clubs, Internazionale Milano or Inter Milan to us brits. The first leg was to be played away at the famous San Siro stadium in Milan, an impressive stadium where no British team had ever beaten Inter. So we had a real uphill task to progress to the Final.

We were very excited, but apprehensive with such a challenge. We arrived in Milan, another wonderful city. On the night of the game, all the nerves melted away as the local fans made sure we didn't have time to worry. We were magnificent on the night and took the game to the defence minded Italians, who were famous for keeping clean sheets at home.

Jimmy Harris scored a belter of a goal to silence the partisan Italian fans and an own goal from the centre half Ballerin clinched a fantastic win, so we became the first English team to taste victory at the San Siro. We didn't need an aeroplane to fly home, we were all on cloud nine, but only half the job was done. For the record, the next English team to win at the San Siro would be Arsenal, some 40 years later.

On 3rd May, the Italians came to St Andrew's, for the second leg. The lights seemed to shine brighter and the fans seemed louder for the great occasion. The prospect of another European Final. The game was a cagey affair, Inter hoping to complete a win, but Jimmy Harris had other ideas and played wonderfully well, scoring two goals in front of 30,000 ecstatic Brummies and we won 2-1, taking the tie 4-2 on aggregate. So we had a final to look forward to, which was to be held next season.

The European nights were really exciting for everybody concerned, from the directors, the players and of course, the fans, who loved to see the continental sides, A C Milan, Inter Milan, A S Roma, Barcelona, European football being quite new to the British. The fans would sing their hearts out with the club song. "Keep right on to the end of the road" would resound round St Andrew's echoing round the ground.

The Final was held up till the following season, September 1961, and we were drawn against another famous Italian team, A S Roma from the Italian capital. The first leg to be played at home. A S Roma arrived at St Andrew's for another cagey game, nerves taking a hold in most of the players, we missed a host of chances and were a bit sloppy in defence and Roma took a 2-0 lead. We got a rollicking at half time and bucked up in the second half. I managed to get a goal which seemed to buck up the whole team. We upped the pace and Jimmy Harris smashed a shot against the bar and Brian Orritt was on hand to knock in the rebound and we ended with a 2-2 draw, a bit lucky but still in the tie.

We travelled to Rome for the second leg which was to be played on 11 October 1961 at the Stadio Olympico, another wonderful stadium. With a crown of over 50,000 Italians screaming for their favourites, the Roma team thoroughly outplayed us and ran out comfortable winners 2-0, thus winning the tie and the trophy 4-2 on aggregate.

Whilst we were in Rome, the roman officials arranged for me to go to St Peter's to see the Pope, Pope John XXIII, a great honour for a catholic boy.

The trophy was presented to the Roma team by Sir Stanley Rous. It was a disappointing end to a wonderful experience.

At the end of that season, we were taken on tour by Birmingham. We went on a six week tour of Canada and America.

In May we had exhibition games against the Scottish side Third Lanark and included a game in the "Big Apple", New York City, which was a real thrill for a lad from the countryside. The buildings were huge, reaching out of sight into the skyline.

The New Yorkers were not into "soccer" as they call it. The national game, baseball, is their thing and the New York Yankees are known worldwide, and American Football is another razzmatazz game, the Americans really like to be entertained.

We also played game in Calgary and Banff, Calgary being famous for the "stampede" a rodeo for the cowboys, although we didn't see it. The country of Canada is a wild and wonderful country, stretching for miles. We seemed to be travel for days between training sessions.

Whilst in Canada, I received news from back in Yorkshire. Because I was on tour, Brenda had gone back to Yorkshire and had given birth to our first child, a son, Laurence, born in Yorkshire in case he grew up to be a cricketer. So I had become a father, and both mother and baby were doing well.

Jack Wiseman, a director at City, arranged a party and a huge cake arrived, much to the delight of all the players and all concerned. I couldn't wait to get back to the UK to see Brenda and my new son.

Back in the UK, I held them so tight they both might break. I was a new father, out of his depth.

CHAPTER 12
CRICKET, LOVELY CRICKET

When we arrived back from Canada, the cricket season was in full swing and I couldn't wait to get my "whites" on and get cracking.

I got a call up to play for Yorkshire 2nds against Cumbria at Penrith Cricket Club. I was down to bat at Number 7 and at number 6 was an impressive young 17 year old lad making his debut, a spindly bespectacled lad, who would go on to have a great career in the game making his first team debut in June 1962 and his England debut in 1964. For Yorkshire, he scored 32,570 runs at an average of 57.85 and played 108 tests for England scoring 8114 runs at an average of 47.72 with 42 centuries and he bowled a bit as well taking 7 test wickets.

I am of course referring to the great Sir Geoffrey Boycott. Who can forget his 100th century against the "old enemy" Australia at Headingley, hitting Greg Chappell for a cracking drive to bring up his century to the delight of 500,000 Yorkshiremen who will tell you they were there when it happened, more like 20,000 but the noise, wow!! How the England test side could do with him now. And to think I batted with him, something to relate to my grandchildren – a claim to fame or what! Trying to get in the Yorkshire side was nearly impossible with the team they had, and youngsters like Boycott coming through.

My football career was getting better and the national press were pushing me to be selected for the England side for the World Cup in Chile, labelling me the "Flying Winger" because of my pace. Walter Winterbottom, the manager, obviously didn't read the papers and I wasn't selected, so I concentrated on the cricket that summer. My mood was lifted when I received an invitation from Warwickshire County Cricket Club, asking if I would play for them. I jumped at the chance as living in Birmingham, locally was ideal. As I said before, trying to get onto the Yorkshire side was virtually impossible.

I played a few games in the second eleven and was chosen to make my first class debut at Edgbaston against Oxford University. This was what I really, really wanted – to play cricket, since I was a kid in short pants, to play the game I loved. To walk out at Edgbaston in Birmingham was the thrill of my life, playing for a County cricket team at a test venue. It doesn't get any better, apart from Yorkshire and Headingley!

I had a very good game, taking six wickets and scoring 60 not out, but this was not enough and didn't keep my place in the first eleven as the regular players who had been rested for the university match returned.

We stayed in Birmingham all that summer and I played for Walsall in the Birmingham League as their professional, and our second child was born, Jane, a "brummie" not a "yorkie".

CHAPTER 13
1962 – A YEAR TO REMEMBER

At the start of the season, Gil Merrick had signed a new left winger from Glasgow Celtic, Bertie Auld, the Scottish International, another speedy player, as tough as nails.

The season started well for me, and I was getting rave write ups in the press. England went to the World Cup without me and had a reasonable tournament, but were eliminated in the quarter finals by the eventual winners Brazil 3-1.

Brazil were brilliant in the competition, playing a new brand of attacking football, a style alien to the British game. Their wingers had freedom to roam wherever they liked, not like the English method, to stay on the wing.

After the "failure" of the World Cup, Walter Winterbottom, the manager, was to try different methods to liven up the England team and make changes to the personnel. The first International of the season was a European qualifier and I received a call up from Walter Winterbottom. I was over the moon, nobody could wipe the smile off my face.

The tie was against France, to be played at Hillsborough, the home of Sheffield Wednesday, a night match under the lights at the Yorkshire ground. I just couldn't believe it, here was a lad from Keighley going to play international football for his country, a lad who only signed for Queens Park Rangers so he could play his beloved cricket in the summer months.

The memories will stay with me forever, sitting in the dressing room with household names, some of whom were to become legends in the 1966 World Cup. Jimmy Armfield made a point of talking to be and calming me down, putting me at my ease.

I was selected and became the 807th man to represent England since the first International match in November 1872. To the present day in 147 years, 1244 players have represented their country. It's still sinking in I think.

3rd October 1962
Hillsborough, Sheffield
7.30pm kick off

England		France	
1.	Ron Springett	1.	Andre Chodra
2.	Jimmy Armfield (Capt.)	2.	Andre Lerond (Capt.)
3.	Bobby Moore	3.	Maryan Synakowski
4.	Maurice Norman	4.	Jean Wending
5.	Ray Wilson	5.	Joseph Benner
6.	Ron Flowers	6.	Rene Ferrier
7.	Mike Hellawell	7.	Raymond Kopa
8.	Chris Crowe	8.	Laurent Robuschi
9.	Alan Hinton	9.	Paul Sauvage
10.	Ray Charnley	10.	Pierre Bernard
11.	Jimmy Greaves	11.	Yvon Goujn

Score 1-1

Flowers (Pen)   Goujon

Attendance 35,380

Jimmy Armfield was a Lancashire lad who had played all his career at his home town Blackpool, making 569 appearances and had played and captained England 43 times, a true gentleman. Bobby Moore, another iconic player, was to make history as the only England Captain to lift the World Cup, a classy half back who had all the time in the world, a wonderful tackler and stylish player. Ray Wilson, was another classy player, a full back with lots of pace and a hard tackle. 1966 was to be another iconic year for him. Jimmy Greaves, the ultimate goal scorer, his name is all you need. He was the best forward I ever played with and against, a natural goal scorer with an electric turn of pace, a silky player.

The game itself was an untidy scrappy affair, a poor game that didn't go to plan and we scraped a 1-1 draw, thanks to a penalty from Ron

Flowers, the cultured centre half. But here was I, a full England International. Wow! I must have done something right as the forward line was completely changed for the next International but myself and Jimmy Greaves kept our places for the next fixture at Windsor Park, Belfast. Walter Winterbottom was getting some pressure from the national press and he seemed to panic and believe he was on borrowed time.

On the plane to Belfast, I was sat next to a journalist/plumber from Preston, who was going to the game for a national newspaper. He was none other than Tom Finney, one of the finest players to ever pull on an England jersey. We chatted the whole way, his knowledge of the game and my career was amazing. He seemed to know all the players and our different styles of play, a true gentleman who wished me luck for the game.

Tom Finney was another player who played all his career for his home-town club Preston North End, 433 games in total and 76 England caps. Bill Shankley once said of Tom "Tom Finney would have been great in any team, in any match, in any age, even if he was wearing an overcoat!", and about a modern player – "Aye, he is nearly as good as Tommy, but then Finney is nearly 60 now!". Praise indeed for a great player.

The crowd at Windsor Park were very vocal and ferocious, patriotic to a man, but we played a good brand of fast attacking football. Jimmy Greaves was magnificent up front and terrified the Northern Ireland defence. I was given a free reign and thought I had a decent game, forcing their keeper to a number of saves on numerous occasions, one shot setting up a goal for Mike O'Grady who scored two goals with Greavesey getting the other in a 3-1 victory.

It turned out I wasn't as good as I thought as I wasn't selected to play again, although I was called up for training.

Sure enough, Walter Winterbottom paid the price for inept performances and a certain Alf Ramsey was brought in to liven up the set up. Alf was in a different league to Walter, with lots of good ideas, team building etc. On my first training session, I was sharing a room with a certain Bobby Charlton, the Manchester United superstar. Bobby was a lovely guy, very charming and quiet. I think the Munich crash altered his life substantially. He was to become one of Britain's most loved players.

Alf Ramsey's methods were totally different to that of Walter Winterbottom. He had studied Brazil in Chile and took ideas from all walks of life. He brought all the players together early for training and team building. He had us working together, eating together and socialising together. We all used to go to the cinema as a group. One of the films he took us to was "This Sporting Life" with Richard Harris and Rachel Roberts, a story of northern life in a rugby league setting. You don't get much tougher than that. Alf seemed to think it settled everybody down, then back to the training centre and supper together. Before I washed up with Alf - he washed the dishes and I dried - this was the nearest I got to being selected for one of his teams. Famously he ditched wingers and look how that turned out.

I liked Alf, a quiet man who looked at you straight in the eye and immediately you knew what he wanted, a man of few words.

When I wasn't selected for the Wales game, my manager went ballistic and slated the selectors in the national press. He believed I had had an outstanding game in Belfast and I was not the only one with a gripe as Mike O'Grady made his debut in that game and scored twice but was not selected again. Imagine the fuss today if one of the young stars did that, there would be public outcry! The papers seem to pick the teams and England caps are awarded for two minute substitute appearances.

Back on the domestic front, we were struggling in the league. We finished in seventeenth place, a point behind Manchester United. We started off well with a 2-1 victory against Fulham, but then went nine games without a win, including a 6-3 stuffing at Wolverhampton Wanderers at home. This was the kick up the backside we needed and we went to Old Trafford to defeat Manchester United 2-0 with myself and Bryan Orritt getting the goals. It was a big thrill to score at the famous Stretford End. This started a good run of games before we were sent crashing back to earth with a 7-1 defeat at Burnley, who were in their prime at that time. Wins away at Manchester City 4-1, where I scored again, Blackburn Rovers and Sheffield United completed the season.

In the FA Cup, we were drawn to play Tottenham Hotspur at home. It turned out to be a cracking cup tie, end to end football from the first whistle. Spurs were an attractive side who played free flowing football. We managed a 3-3 draw, and left the fans drooling over the replay at White Hart Lane. The replay was another six goal thriller, but this time we lost 4-2.

INTER CITIES FAIRS CUP

Because we reached the final the previous year, we automatically qualified for this year's competition. We were drawn against the Spanish side Espanol, the first leg to be played in Barcelona on 15th November 1961.

To say we got stuffed was something of an understatement, in front of 60,000 fanatical Spaniards, we were soundly thrashed 5-2, Diego Coups scoring a hat-trick, with the two Jimmies, Bloomfield and Harris, replying for us. The second leg at St Andrew's was a really bad tempered affair, players hacking at each other from the word go. Both teams finished with nine players, Jimmy Harris and Bertie Auld being sent off for us and the game ended a 1-0 win but an aggregate loss 5-3.

We didn't fare much better in the League Cup, losing to Swindon Town 2-0 after a 1-1 stalemate at home. I played in every game that season, a total of 50 appearances.

CHAPTER 14
1962-63 HISTORY FOR THE BLUE

After a red hot summer playing cricket, we returned to Birmingham for the new season. This was to be an iconic season for Birmingham City. It was City's 60th season in the Football League and their 36th in the First Division.

The League campaign started disastrously and we went the first five games without a win, having had three tough away games at Tottenham Hotspur, Arsenal and Manchester United, losing them all. Two home draws left us at the bottom of the table and a fight against relegation was already on the cards.

The next game was against Burnley and at last we clicked, winning 5-1 with myself getting two goals. Another three games were to follow including a 5-0 thumping by Sheffield Wednesday - the Owls were on fire that day - and then another drubbing at Upton Park, Wests Ham United putting five past us with no reply. We had to buck up our ideas and work harder and train harder.

The extra effort began to show fruit and we went on a six match unbeaten spell, including a 5-1 win at Portman Road, the home of Ipswich Town, before crashing back down to earth at home losing to Liverpool 2-0.

We were now dragged into a dog fight at the foot of the table and went eleven games without a win, 6 defeats and 5 draws. A win at home to West Ham United eased the bad feeling around the club, but not for long as we were torn apart at Anfield losing 5-1 to Liverpool. With three games to go until the season conclusion, we needed two victories to secure our First Division status.

The first of the three "cup finals" was Manchester United at home, a hard fought win gave us hope, one down, one to go. The following week, we travelled to Turf Moor, the home of Burnley, a small tight ground suited to Burnley's styles of play and it turned out a win for Burnley 3-1. So the last game of the season was Leicester City at home, nerves were frazzled to breaking point, but we succeeded in a 3-2 victory and escaped relegation by two points ahead of Manchester City and the already doomed Leyton Orient.

October 1962

The whole world held its breath as the two world superpowers USA and USSR were embroiled in an escapade involving Cuba, the "Bay of Pigs", as it was to be known, a missile crisis. Finally the two world powers managed to sort it out. President J F Kennedy and President Khrushchev got together at the last minute with Fidel Castro to avert disaster.

Our relegation issues seemed a bit trivial at the time in comparison.

FA Cup

1963 was one of the coldest on record and instead of the third round being traditionally played in January, because of the extreme frost and postponed games, the round was played on 5th March.

We were drawn against Bury on a still frozen pitch and were lucky to get away with a 3-3 draw in front of nearly 40,000 fans. It seemed their fans had missed their Saturday dose of football. We were well beaten in the replay at the tiny Gigg Lane ground, 2-0 the final score.

Because of the freezing winter, we missed a total of ten weeks of play. There was no under-soil heating in those days, just the frozen rutted mud. In fact the game against Bury was postponed a total of fourteen times! Winters! The youngsters of today have never seen a winter!

League Cup

Before the big freeze set in, we were down to play Doncaster Rovers at home on 24th September. All the troubles of our league campaign disappeared as if the brakes had been taken off and we walloped Rovers 5-0.

In the next round, we drew Barrow from Cumbria, the game was to be played on their small compact ground and they played as if they were after a money spinning replay at St Andrews. They parked the bus, as they say and got a creditable 1-1 draw. In the replay, on a much bigger playing surface, the Barrow lads were stretched to capacity and we were given lots of space and won quite easily 5-1.

On 14th November, we entertained Notts County and another tight game. Eventually we ran out 3-2 winners and considered ourselves a trifle lucky. Out league form was like a yoyo but we seemed to relax in the League Cup.

Our next opponents in the fifth round were Manchester City at home. They too were struggling in the league and we ended up thrashing them 6-0, thus taking us to the semi-final. This was to be a two legged affair against Bury, who had just knocked us out of the FA Cup, so revenge was on the cards.

The first leg of the semi-final was played at home and both teams went head to head, a full blooded attacking game and we managed to score three times to Bury's two. So everything to hinge on the second leg.

On 8th April 1963, at Gigg Lane, Bury, holding a one goal advantage, we made a cagey defensive start and Bury threw the kitchen sink at us, on a mud bath of a pitch. Both defences were solid and few mistakes were made. We were thoroughly professional and came away with a 1-1 draw and an aggregate win by the odd goal, and we were in the final.

In those days, there was no showpiece Wembley moneymaking final. The final was played over two legs, home and away. Who were we to play in the final? None other than our city neighbours and greatest rivals Aston Villa.

"The Villa versus The Blues"
2nd City Derby!

23rd May 1963

The first leg of an emotional final was to be played under the lights at St Andrews. 32,000 Brummies packed the ground, a "private" Birmingham affair. Brummies were either "Blues" or "Villas" and the noise was deafening, like most nights under the floodlights.

We started quite well and took the lead when Jimmy Harris fed Bertie Auld, who crossed for Ken Leek, who scored with a powerful shot, silencing the "Villans". Not long after, Bobby Thompson equalised, so the score was 1-1 at half time. So after a slice of orange and a cup of tea, a quick drag in the toilets for the smokers, we were back out into the cauldron.

Seven minutes into the second half, Jimmy and Bertie worked their magic again and Ken Leek a second goal and a 2-1 lead. We looked a little more relaxed now, but Villa were playing on the break and were always a threat. Nigel Sims was having a blinder in the Villa goal, but on 66 minutes, Jimmy Bloomfield got the ball and went on a jinking mazy run, beating three defenders before shooting from a really tight angle. The ball zoomed in to make the score 3-1 to the Blues and all was set up for a rip roaring second leg.

The Second leg of the Final was played at Villa Park on 27th May 1963. Villa Park was packed to the rafters and the "Villans" were up to knock us out of our stride.
We travelled by coach through the packed streets, the short distance to Villa Park with a defensive strategy in mind to hold onto our lead. We set up in a defensive mould and I would put in more tackles in one night than the rest of the season.

The defence was magnificent with Captain Trevor Smith outstanding. We tried every trick in the book to run the clock down, much to the infuriation of Villa players and fans alike. It worked a treat. Aston Villa couldn't get into a rhythm at all, and the game died a death, a complete 0-0 stalemate, but it was as good as a 10-0 win as we had done the job and we were the cup winners. The crowd invaded the pitch at full time, to celebrate with the players. The first piece of silverware that Birmingham City had ever won, and to do it at the home of our biggest rivals was the icing on the cake. We had a cup of tea and a bun to celebrate and champagne in our commemorative tankards. It was a great way to end the season, and fans and players partied well into the night.

That summer was one of the hottest on record – cold winters, hot summers.

Mike
Hollowell

My 1963 A&BC Football Card

League Cup Final 1st leg
23rd March 1963
St Andrews
Attendance 31,580

Birmingham City	v	Aston Villa
1. Johnny Schofield		1. Nigel Sims
2. Stan Lynn		2. Cammie Fraser
3. Colin Green		3. Charlie Aitken
4. Terry Hennessey		4. Vic Crowe
5. Trevor Smith (C)		5. John Sleeuwenhoek
6. Malcolm Beard		6. Gordon Lee
7. Mike Hellawell		7. Alan Baker
8. Jimmy Bloomfield		8. George Graham
9. Jimmy Harris		9. Bobby Thomson
10. Ken Leek		10. Ron Wylie
11. Bertie Auld		11. Harry Burrows
Manager Gil Merrick		Manager Joe Mercer

Birmingham City 3

Leek 14,52

Bloomfield 66

Aston Villa 1

Thomson 83

League Cup Final 2nd leg
27th May 1963
Villa Park
Attendance 37,921

Aston Villa	v	Birmingham City
1. Nigel Sims		1. Johnny Schofield
2. Cammie Fraser		2. Stan Lynn
3. Charlie Aitken		3. Colin Green
4. Vic Crowe		4. Terry Hennessey
5. Lew Chatterley		5. Trevor Smith (C)
6. Gordon Lee		6. Malcolm Beard
7. Alan Baker		7. Mike Hellawell
8. George Graham		8. Jimmy Bloomfield
9. Bobby Thomson		9. Jimmy Harris
10. Ron Wyllie		10. Ken Leek
11. Harry Burrows		11. Bertie Auld

Manager Joe Mercer

Manager Gil Merrick

Aston Villa 0   **Birmingham City 0**

CHAPTER 15
1963 – A YEAR FOR THE WHOLE WORLD

The new Season was supposed to be the start of something good, we were still in the First Division, a new beginning and we were cup holders. We looked forward with anticipation.

We started at Bolton Wanderers at home and won the game 2-1 with a penalty from Stan Lynn and a tap in from myself. However, this victory was followed by successive defeats away at Leicester City and Fulham. The next game was at home against Leicester City on 11th September 1963 and I remember it as if it was yesterday.

Playing in goal for Leicester City was a certain Gordon Banks, who was to become a national icon in 1966 and a national favourite, and one of the greatest goalkeepers England have ever had. A World Cup winner and a lovely, lovely man. I had travelled with him for England and he used to tease me that my left leg was only used for standing on and I only had one foot.

During the game, he kept telling the Leicester full back Richie Norman, who was marking me, to let me go down the inside as I couldn't kick with my left. Later in the game I came up against Richie for the umpteenth time, I cut inside him and let fly from fully 35 yards (it gets further every year!) with my "standing" foot (a fluke I think) but I caught it fully at it screamed into the top corner past a despairing dive from Gordon, like a guided missile. That was probably the best goal I ever scored and against the legendary Gordon Banks (Pete couldn't do that!)

Every time I saw Gordon after that, he teased me rotten, telling me it was a fluke and that if I tried it a million times, I would never do it again!

A lovely man, and a true gentleman. God bless you Gordon.

After a draw at Old Trafford, we lost three games on the trot before a win at Ipswich Town, then a run of four consecutive defeats. We were now in November and the winter was beginning to look bleak. A win against Chelsea eased the pressure on the team and the manager Gil Merrick. We were twentieth in the league and relegation once again was a serious threat.

November 1963 was to be a date in history that everybody in the world would remember. Another "I can remember where I was on that day" moment. The 22nd November became infamous for whilst driving through the streets of Dallas, Texas, the President of the United States of America was shot and assassinated. John Fitzgerald Kennedy was slain by a gunman while sitting next to his wife Jacqueline in an open top car, and the whole thing was shown on television, as was the subsequent capture of the gunman Lee Harvey Oswald and then his shooting by Jack Ruby. It could only happen in America.

The whole things dragged on for weeks like a Hollywood soap. Everybody was glued to their TVs and the talk of conspiracy and counter conspiracies goes on until this day. Kennedy was a charismatic character, cajoling and goading the USSR, starting with the Space Race. The USSR were to win the battle into space with the first man Yuri Gagarin, but the USA countered with John Glenn. Then with the Bay of Pigs crisis, the world watched in wonder and a little fear. So when Kennedy was assassinated, many people looked towards the USSR for answers. Tensions between the two countries were at a high. After 1969 when the USA "won" the race to the moon, the tensions got easier and now they work together on various programmes.

Who can forget Neil Armstrong's words "Once small step for man, one giant leap for mankind." Who knows what the future holds.

The day after the assassination, we were due to play Nottingham Forest, but the game took second thoughts with both fans and players and a 3-3 draw was the result, but I doubt that any fan can remember the game.

We just couldn't get a winning run going. We had good results, wins against West Ham United and Manchester United, but these were few and far between, and we remained in the bottom three.

1964 came in and things got even worse, with a run of eight defeats in a row and a trip to our arch rivals Aston Villa next. We seemed to be up for the local derby and travelled to Villa Park and won 3-0 with me scuffing one in.

Another three defeats in a row saw us drop to twenty first place, with only two games to go, both at home and must win games to stay in the Division or at least have a chance. Two cup finals, the supporters were magnificent and became our twelfth man. We saw off Liverpool 3-1 and finished the season with a 3-0 win over Sheffield United and finished twentieth position, one point ahead of Bolton Wanderers and Ipswich Town.

This league position was not good enough for the directors who thought that Birmingham City were a big city team who had just won the league cup and should be at the top of the league, not the bottom. So in June, the manager was told the bad news that his services were no longer required. Gil Merrick left under a cloud and the media and Gil himself were very upset. Gil was a legend at the club, having served for 25 years as a player and manager. In the future, the club would rename a stand after him.

Joe Mallett was appointed the new manager. Joe had been reserve team coach at Nottingham Forest. Many in the media thought that this job was too much for an untried manager, as he had no experience of management, especially a big city First Division club. Joe had been a player for Southampton, making 215 appearances, a tough tackling wing half.

FA Cup

We were drawn against Port Vale at home and our league form was obvious and we were knocked out 2-1.

League Cup

As holders, we were considered a scalp for every other team. We were drawn against Norwich City at Carrow Road. They treated the game as their cup final and were easy 2-0 winners.

Another poor season for the Blues. This season saw the start of the iconic football programme on the BBC, Match of the Day. This first football programme is still going strong.

CHAPTER 16
ON THE MOVE

The 1964-65 season was to be a landmark for me. Gil Merrick, a good friend and manager had gone and Joe Mallett took his place. He decided he needed a new outlook for the team and we were to play more defensively. He had no time for wingers, which made me obsolete in his mind and plans.

We started the season worse than before under Gil, with two draws and four defeats, leaving us twentieth in the Division. We won a couple of games in September which lifted us up to seventeenth. It didn't last and here we were fighting relegation. Joe was a bit out of his depth. I didn't fit in with his plans, if there were any plans. The players had their doubts and morale was very low.

In December we played Sunderland who had just been promoted that year. I had a cracking game, laying on three of the four goals we scored in a 4-3 win. But then back to normal. After the busy Christmas period, I was summoned to the office of Walter Adams, the Birmingham City secretary. He told me that Sunderland, who together with Leeds United had been promoted that year, had been in touch with regards to signing me, and he asked if I was interested in talking to them. As I didn't seem to fit in with Joe's plans, I thought what had I got to lose, so I agreed to travel to Sunderland to talk to their manager.

A rail tip up the spectacular East Coat with the views of the North Sea was wonderful, and I arrived at the home of Sunderland, Roker Park. George Hardwick was the manager. He had been a tough tackling left back at rivals Middlesbrough, making 143 appearances. A local lad from Saltburn on Sea who had also played 190 times for Oldham Athletic and played for England 13 times. A statue or George now stands outside the Riverside, the new home of Middlesbrough.

He was a quietly spoken gentleman who spoke slowly and told me all about his plans for playing attacking, attractive football with speedy wingers, providing the crosses for the attacking players, a total difference to Joe Mallett's concept of football. I had obviously made an impression with my performance against Sunderland the previous month.

He "sold" me his ideas of joining a club who had the most passionate fans and the "Roker Roar" was spine chilling to opponents and "Haway the lads" beaming out. So when he offered a salary of £30 per week and a bonus of £20 per point, I was getting my pen out. At that time the salary was amazing. He said he would contact Birmingham City and I was to come back in a week's time to formalise the contract. It felt good to be wanted again.

When I got home and told Brenda, she could see the change in my mood immediately. We were told by Sunderland that a club house would be provided for our accommodation and I should bring Brenda with me to look at it then when I had finally finalised the contract.

Our family was growing fast and Laurence and Jane were joined by another girl Anne. Brenda had her hands full but agreed to get her parents to come down from Yorkshire to look after the children while we made the trip to the North East. Brenda's mum and dad duly arrived from Keighley and we took the Newcastle train up the North East coast, wondering what was in store and who Sunderland would send to meet us off the train.

When the train pulled in to the station, a huge shock and surprise was to await us. On the platform was none other than a certain Brian Clough. Brian was a blunt, brash, gruff Yorkshireman who was never short of a comment. He was injured at the time, with a knee injury that would end his career at his peak. He'd had 274 appearances (213 for Middlesbrough and 61 for Sunderland) scoring an incredible 251 goals and two appearances for England. He was to make his name as a manager with the help of Peter Taylor. Together they formed a formidable partnership and won titles with Derby County and two European cups with Nottingham Forest. He even took the job at Leeds United after Don Revie had left, but his blunt style didn't go down well with the established stars at United and the directors dispensed with his services after 44 days.

Brenda wasn't impressed by the blunt talking Clough. After showing us around various club houses we reached a three bedroomed semi-detached house. Cloughie extolled the virtues of the house as if he owned it, pointing out the good points and disregarding the bad points, such as broken panes of glass and a crack in the bath. We were not impressed at all, and Brian grunted "What's up with it?" to which Brenda retorted "Would you live in it?" Cloughie was stunned into silence, maybe the only time he was lost for words!

1-0 to Brenda.

We eventually found a house in Leechmere Road, Tunstall, which would be available in 10-12 weeks, so until then we stayed at the Roker Hotel on the front.

I made my debut for Sunderland at Roker Park against Blackpool. I could not believe the volume of noise that came off the stands. It was deafening. The famous "Roker Roar" lifted the home players until we felt ten feet tall and made the opposition into shrinking violets. They were the "twelfth man" and made Roker Park a fortress.

Luckily our home record pulled us through the season. This was Sunderland's first season in the First Division after promotion and some of the games were really hard against the established more experienced teams. We finished the season in a creditable fifteenth position, some ten points better than my previous side Birmingham City, who were relegated to the Second Division, thus justifying my decision to move clubs and it also resulted in my previous manager, Joe Mallett losing his job after just one season.

I was made so welcome by the fans and players of Sunderland and friendships were made which are still as strong today. Sunderland was and is a football daft city. Wherever I went, shopping with Brenda, I was stopped and asked for autographs (no selfies in those days). Everybody knew who I was, unlike the bigger city Birmingham, where I could wander round and only the most ardent of fans knew me.

I made 14 appearances until the end of the season, a quarter season, and scored a couple of goals.

Life was good, the house was ready and the cricket season was here. So we moved in with Brenda's parents in Keighley and I played cricket for the town club, and Brenda could catch up with all the family.

During the summer I received a big shock. George Hardwick, the manager, who persuaded me to up roots to the North East, and filled me with his ideas of flying wingers and attacking football, had been sacked by the directors of Sunderland. Seemingly fifteenth position was not good enough for them.

The directors replaced George with the former Scottish international Ian McColl, who had made his name at Glasgow Rangers, making 362 appearances, and was the current Scotland manager. He had had great success with the national side with impressive wins against England, both home and away, and a 6-2 win against Spain in Madrid, and a 6-1 win against Northern Ireland at Windsor Park. Ian came down from Scotland and brought the classy wing half Jim Baxter with him from Glasgow Rangers. Jim, unfortunately, was recovering from a bad leg fracture and was no longer the "slim Jim" of his Glasgow days. The skill was still there but he pace had gone. Jim was the darling of the Ibrox fans. He was known for being a joker on the pitch. His ability and vision often sent opponents the wrong was to the delight of the supporters, like a matador with a bull. He also broke an unwritten tradition by becoming friends with the Glasgow Celtic players, "the old enemy". This was taboo in those days, Protestants mixing with Catholics was a no no. Unfortunately Jim played hard off the field as well as on, and he was on the front pages of the newspapers more than being on the sports pages. His best days were behind him, but Ian thought he could bring something special to Sunderland. The catholic players at Sunderland held their breath when Ian strolled into Roker Park, especially Charlie Hurley, the "king" of Sunderland and a staunch catholic. Their fears became reality when Ian began picking the team on religious grounds, rather than ability, but the Roker fans took to Jim Baxter as he thrilled the Roker faithful with skills of a juggler. He could make the ball talk, but his fitness was nowhere near and the opponents knew it.

The season was a topsy turvy affair, good wins and disastrous losses. On 6th September 1965, I made Sunderland history. At the start of the season, the Football League introduced substitutes for the first time, and on the 6th September I was pulled off and replaced by Alan Garden, a question that was to be asked on Mastermind! Another claim to fame, but one I didn't really want, must have had a stinker that day.

Our home form was poor and not even the Roker Roar could lift us. The away form was even worse, winning just one game away all season at Bloomfield Road, Blackpool. We were really struggling and Ian McColl was chopping and changing the side, too much I thought, but he was trying everything. Neil Martin was brought in to bolster the side, another Scot to steady the ship. I was in and out of the side and soon realised I didn't fit in with Ian's plan, he wasn't keen on wingers.

In the FA cup we were drawn away at Goodison Park and were well beaten by Everton. In the League Cup, we started with a win against Sheffield United, but were soundly beaten by our bogey team Aston Villa. But a festival of football was coming to England and Roker Park was to play host to various nations and their fans from across the world for the 1966 FIFA World Cup.

My 1964 card and a later one below

MIKE HELLAWELL
(Birmingham)

CHAPTER 17
A FESTIVAL OF FOOTBALL

The whole of England came to a standstill for a month of football in 1966.

The whole world had come to England to enjoy the festivities. Roker Park was to host three games in the qualifying stage, along with eight other grounds across England. Italy, Chile and the USSR were to be treated to the Roker Roar.

Roker Park and the surrounding houses all got in the spirit of the tournament. Bunting and flags were at every house and ground across England, but what the Chileans, Italians and Russians made of the Wearsiders and the "why aye man" and "Ha'way, canny, gannin", I don't know. The universal language of football won in the end.

The other grounds hosting the tournament were Wembley and White City in London; Hillsborough and Villa Park in the Midlands; Old Trafford and Goodison Park in the North West; and Roker Park and Ayresome Park in the North East. So as many fans as possible were to see the games and over a million fans turned out.

All the games were shown on TV so everybody could watch the cream of world football and not miss a kick. The whole population breathed, watched and talked football for the whole of July, a summer festival of football. We all watched the games and revelled in the skills of Pele of Brazil, probably the greatest player the world had ever seen. Pele scored over 1,000 goals for his home team Santos and Brazil. Eusebio of Portugal, who was to be the tournament's leading goal scorer, the Benfican striker, had a wonderful tournament, to name just a couple.

As the tournament progressed, there were big shocks. North Korea, the minnows, managed to beat the giants of Italy at Ayresome Park Middlesbrough, thus eliminating one of the favourites. Pele and his Brazilian maestros were kicked off the park at Goodison by a cynical Bulgarian side and eventually the odds on favourites were knocked out by Hungary 3-1.

Portugal, who were making their first appearance at the finals, had made quite an impact and won all their group games. Eusebio scored 9 goals to win the "golden boot", a great player and a terrific sportsman.

The usual suspects qualified for the knockout rounds: West Germany, Argentina, Portugal and Hungary, the dark horses who sent the favourites back to Brazil early. In the North East, USSR and the minnows North Korea qualified, thus sending another favourite Italy back home.

The games at Roker were:

Italy 2 – Chile 0

USSR 1 – Italy 0

USSR 2 – Chile 1

The three nations playing with "The Roker Roar" and "Haway the lads" ringing in their ears.

Meanwhile in the capital, London, England had enjoyed home advantage, being the hosts of the competition, and were progressing nicely under my washing up partner Alf Ramsey. After a 0-0 stalemate and an ugly game against Uruguay, they played Mexico at Wembley and a brace from my roommate Bobby Charlton, one an absolute thunderbolt I would have been proud of, secured a 2-0 win. Next up for England was France and a couple of goals from Roger Hunt, the Liverpool centre forward, was enough to seal progress from the qualifying games and into the knockout stage and a date with Argentina in front of 90,000 fans.

The game itself was a bad tempered game with Argentinians trying every trick in the book to knock England out of their stride, kicking every player wearing the Three Lions. The Argentinian captain went too far with physical approach and was rightly sent off. This gave England a man advantage and Geoff Hurst (who had been a late replacement for the injured Jimmy Greaves) scored the only goal of the game, and England were in the semi-final.

The other quarter finals were more straightforward. West Germany eased past Uruguay 4-0 at Hillsborough and Roker Park hosted the USSR versus Hungary, the USSR winning 2-1. The last quarter final was an exciting affair played at Goodson Park, Liverpool. The minnows of North Korea were playing Portugal. The North Koreans shocked everybody by scoring in the first minute and followed up, scoring two more to lead 3-0 and were cruising. But naivety set in and instead of holding on, they kept attacking, leaving gaps at the back and the Portuguese took advantage and the fabulous Eusebio scored twice before half-time. The second half saw normality resumed with Eusebio scoring two more and Portugal ran out 5-3 winners to book a semi-final spot against the hosts England. The North Koreans went home with the hearts of every fan, they played their football with big smiles, big hearts, and made millions of new fans.

The first semi-final at Goodison Park was a tight cagey affair with West Germany coming out close winners against the USSR 2-1, Franz Beckonbauer, the classy West German running the game. The next night at Wembley, England took on Portugal, a wonderful occasion under the floodlights. The whole nation watched on TV and 95,000 were captivated at the ground. The imperious Bobby Charlton was at his magnificent best scoring twice before that man Eusebio pulled one back from the penalty spot. England won the game 2-1 and were in the final. At the final whistle, the Portuguese players and especially Eusebio, were the first to hug and congratulate the England players, true sportsmen to a man.

The third place play off at Wembley drew an amazing crowd of 88,000 and that man Eusebio scored again along with the giant centre forward Torres to win the tie 2-1 against a resilient USSR team.

So now the whole nation was on pins waiting for the 30th July and the final, in front of Her Majesty the Queen. We were so lucky at Sunderland as the directors had secured tickets to the final for the players and their wives. We were to have a superb weekend in London and catch the game as well. What a bonus, players and "WAGS" as they are known today.

We went as a group to London by train and the whole city was awash with fans and expectations. We stayed in a hotel and had a great "tourist" time, wining and dining. The Scots in the Sunderland squad were happy to enjoy the occasion, but they all wanted West Germany to prevail over the "auld enemy", such was the rivalry then.

The match and the occasion was a magnificent affair, nobody does pomp like the Brits. The team from Germany got off to a flyer and Helmut Haller scored to take an early lead. Geoff Hurst had kept his place, even though Jimmy Greaves was fit again. After some great play by Bobby Moore taking a quick free kick, Geoff rose the highest to head in the equaliser, a West Ham goal if ever I saw one. So the game stayed in a stalemate end to end but no clear chances, but then a blunder in the German defence saw Martin Peters knock in a bouncing ball. Peters was a star in the making, another West Ham player.

All looked well for England and the fans were getting ready to celebrate, when with just minutes to go, the ball pinged about like a snooker ball in the England area and Wolfgang Weber pounced before Ray Wilson and Jackie Charlton, and his the equaliser past Gordon Banks. Knocking the wind out of the souls of the players and the nation's fans, the game was now destined for extra time. The German tactics were working perfectly with Franz Beckenbauer man marking Bobby Charlton out of the game, but thus negating his own contribution. In extra time Geoff Hirst tried and shot in one movement, the ball hitting the bar and crossing the line (according to the Russian linesman) but even with modern technology doubts remain to this day, but as we say in Yorkshire, look at the scoreboard – 3-2 it read. The West Germans now threw caution to the wind, looking for an equaliser, and in the very last minute of the game, Geoff Hurst broke away and smashed the ball into the net for a 4-2 score and a hat-trick for Geoff, the first ever in a world cup final, thus making Alf Ramsey's selection of Geoff over Jimmy, perfect. The final whistle went and England had won the World Cup for the first time, the Jules Rimet Cup, and the nation on TV were treated to "Some people are on the pitch, they think it's all over. It is now!" The now immortal words of the commentator Kenneth Wolstenholme. Who hasn't' heard those words?

The trophy had gone missing some months earlier when on show, at an exhibition and was found in a hedge by a dog named "Pickles" who was to become as famous as the players and is now a question in many a pub quiz. The Jules Rivet trophy of solid gold was presented to the England captain Bobby Moore by Her Majesty the Queen.

Who can forget the scenes after the game, the players running round the pitch displaying the trophy, Nobby Stiles dancing and jogging round, minus his teeth. It was a fabulous occasion and all the pubs were busy for days after, expectations were very high and the future of English football looked bright.

1966 while playing for Sunderland and below against Blackburn Rovers

CHAPTER 18
HUDDERFIELD HERE I COME

Expectations were equally as high at Sunderland, the euphoria was countrywide, and after the success of Alf Ramsey's wingless wonders, wingers were becoming a thing of the past and everybody was starting to play the Ramsey way 4-4-3. I was in and out of the first team and in October, I was informed that Huddersfield Town were now interested in signing me (A team I had played for at junior level, and who rejected me on the advice of their coach Bill Shankley who thought I was too frail and wouldn't "make it"). Huddersfield Town were a Second Division side riding high in the league and pushing for promotion. My immediate thoughts went back to 1955 when my father had asked if they wanted to sign me and they said "no thanks". Now they wanted to pay a transfer fee for me, funny old world.

Tom Johnson was the manager of Town. He knew me from my time at Birmingham City where he was a coach. He had had a playing career with Peterborough United, Nottingham Forest and Notts County. Huddersfield Town were a mixture of seasoned professionals and up and coming youngsters. Jimmy Nicholson from Manchester United, an Irish International, Colin Dobson from Sheffield Wednesday, Trevor Cherry, a young player who was to go on to be an England International and star for Leeds United, and a fine centre forward in Tony Leighton.

I didn't take much time in thinking of signing as I was a Yorkshire lad and Huddersfield was only a stone's throw from my hometown, Keighley. The playing surface at Leeds Road was huge, just perfect for a winger with lots of pace to exploit. In my time there I must have explored every blade of grass.

My 1967 card

Just recently I was talking to a Town fan and he told me the Town fans nicknamed me "Arkle" after the famous steeplechaser. The Irish racehorse was winning everything together with his jockey Pat Taffe. Who can forget the epic duels with the other horse Mill House in the Cheltenham Gold Cup? Although Arkle used to jump the fences, not the full back's legs!

My one big regret about my time at Huddersfield Town was I didn't score enough goals. When I did score, the rest of the lads made a big fuss and got the Press down to Leeds Road to celebrate.

We were pushing for promotion to the First Division and were having a good season until the final stages, when we couldn't buy a win. We lost five games out of the last ten and missed out on promotion finishing sixth. In the FA Cup we played Chelsea at home in the third round and lost 2-1, and we fared about the same in the League Cup, getting beaten by Lincoln City at the first time of asking. In total, I made 32 appearances, but only managed one goal, a poor season for me really.

The following season everybody was expecting us to make the next step and push for promotion, but the opposite occurred, we were very poor, our league form was iffy to say the least. We started with two wins at Bristol City and at home to Millwall, then we had five defeats in seven games and then a mixture of wins and losses, we couldn't string a run together and a poor season resulted in us finishing fourteenth in the league. We were beaten 2-1 away at Tranmere Rovers in the FA Cup with a young up and coming star Frank Worthington scoring our goal.

Frank Worthington was a young lad with a great future. I used to pick him up at Shelf on the way to training. Frank was to become a great player with a host of clubs including Leeds, Leicester, Southampton, and my old clubs Birmingham City and Sunderland to name just a few, scoring 260 goals in a long career and playing for England on eight occasions when at Leicester City. Frank is now battling Alzheimer's disease and I wish him well.

Like at Birmingham City in 1963, the League Cup became a relaxing competition away from our league form. In the Cup we seemed much freer in our position and played with more freedom. In the first round, we defeated Wolverhampton Wanderers at home 1-0, Colin Dobson scoring and next up was Norwich City at Carrow Road, another 1-0 win with Jimmy Nicholson getting the all-important goal.

Next up West Ham United at Leeds Road and we ran out easy winners with young Frank Worthington and Chris Cattlin getting on the scoresheet, 2-0 final score. Fulham were next and we travelled to Craven Cottage by the Thames for the fixture and managed a 2-1 win with Jimmy Nicholson and Shaw scoring for us.

So here we were in another semi-final, a two legged tie against yet another London club, Arsenal. In front of 40,000 Londoners, we put up a good scrap, with the Highbury faithful cheering on their team to a close 3-2 win. Trevor Cherry and Colin Dobson replying for Town. So the second leg was an uphill task but we went at the Arsenal, however they were too strong and won 3-1, thus 6-3 on aggregate. So the dream of two League Cup winner's medals was gone.

The directors of the club had pinned all their hopes on promotion, not the Cups and this was to cost Tom Johnson his job. The club sacked Tom and replaced him with Ian Greaves, the former Manchester United player. He too was a 4-4-3 formation man and he didn't have much time for wingers.

I loved my time at Huddersfield Town. The supporters were magnificent, but I didn't fit into their style of play and I was out of favour. In October Norman Rigby, the manager of Peterborough United asked me if I would sign for them. He outlined his plans to pay with wingers, so I was on the move again. I made my Peterborough United debut at Southend United on the south coast. Southend is famous for having the longest pier in the world with its own rail line for tourists to get to the end. We lost the game on the Saturday and Norman was sacked on the Monday. I must be a jinx on managers! They don't last long, it's the name of the game. Results count and directors have no patience.

Jim Iley was appointed as successor to Norman. Jim had had a long career playing 545 games for Sheffield United, Tottenham Hotspur, Nottingham Forest, Newcastle United and Peterborough. Another 4-3-3 man (here we go again) and he told me from the start he had no time for wingers, so going to Peterborough was going to bite me on the backside and I ended only making 9 appearances.

The football "dream" was now dying a death, so we had to prepare for life after football. Brenda and I bought a small newsagents shop in Keighley to cater for our futures. Then out of the blue, a sudden twist of fate. Gil Merrick, my manager at Birmingham City got in touch and asked if I wanted to stay in football. He was now the manager of a non-league club in the Midlands, who were very progressive and ambitious. Bromsgrove Rovers, a club in Worcestershire. Gil informed me that I could remain in Keighley and travel down to Bromsgrove to play at weekends, thus playing part-time and still run the shop in Keighley with Brenda and Auntie Mary.

He asked if my brother John would come as well. John had played professionally for Bradford City, Rotherham United, Darlington and Bradford Park Avenue and was a left winger. This suited us both as we could both travel down together. We both agreed and Gil said he would sort everything out.

I was playing cricket for the Hawks XI at a beautiful cricket ground in the Yorkshire Dales when Gil emerged with his wife and the papers. Settle Cricket Club was the setting for signing for Bromsgrove, a nicer place you couldn't wish for. Gil and his wife enjoyed the journey to the Dales and made a short holiday of the occasion.

We both played for Bromsgrove for two years until father time told me I was getting slower and the travelling was getting time consuming and cousin Pamela was having to help in the shop on Saturdays. By now we had another addition to the family, a boy Richard, another birth in Yorkshire so he could play for the county of his birth, just in case. In those days only Yorkshiremen could play for Yorkshire.

The newsagents was thriving and was providing a living and so I decided to retire from football and concentrate on family life. Brenda was run ragged by the four children and needed a hand. The newsagents was a seven day week job and if I wanted to play cricket at the weekend I had to employ staff or get relatives in, so when the next door shop became vacant, we decided to make a fresh start, ditching the news agency and starting up a greengrocer's. So I became a greengrocer, a jack of all trades, but as Brenda says "a master of none"!

Since I became a professional footballer at the age of 17, I had wanted for nothing. If I needed a doctor, the club would send one, if I needed a plumber, the club would send one. The same with the butcher, the baker and candlestick maker, so when I finished playing, I had not a clue how to make an appointment or do a job myself.

I wasn't a practical man and had no idea about DIY. The only time I looked after myself was when I was in the Army and washing up with Sir Alf Ramsey. So here I was, let loose in Keighley, getting up early to go to the market and selling fruit and veg to the poor unsuspecting folk.

The greengrocers kept us fed and watered until 1987. Large supermarkets were springing up in town and undercutting the "little man" who couldn't compete and the smaller shops began to struggle. I was 49 and I decided for the first time I would have to get a "proper job" to look after my family.

I ended up finding a job for a mail order company in Bingley, about four miles from home, the famous thermal wear producer, Damart, where I sorted mail in the office. I found it hard at first to do a normal job, turning up every day, clocking on, doing a job, clocking off, doing office work in a busy environment, just like my conscription days.

One day at Damart, one of the managers called me telling me a rep wanted to talk to me. I didn't usually see any reps from other companies, but the manager insisted. I went into the office and the rep waiting for me was no other than Denis Law, the "king" of Manchester United and the darling of the Stretford End. Denis and I had crossed swords many times on the football field and we spent a couple of hours reminiscing about the football of the 60's. Denis was one of the "holy trinity" of Best, Law and Charlton with a statue of the three outside Old Trafford.

Denis had begun his career at Huddersfield Town and was transferred to Manchester City for £55,000, a British record at the time. He only played one season at City and was sold to Torino in Italy for £110,000, another record for a British player. He didn't settle in Italy and Matt Busby persuaded him to join Manchester United for £115,000, early a day's wages for some modern players of today. Denis spent eleven years at United, nicknamed the "king" and the "Lawman", by the fans. He won the FA Cup in his first year, scoring against Leicester City and won the League titles. He also won the Ballon D'Or for the best player in the world in 1964. Denis was a great goal scorer and an avid Scotsman.

Another special visitor to the company was Princess Diana on 12 September 1991. She arrived with little pomp, but the beautiful princess captivated everyone with her down-to-earth approach, having time for all the staff and the crowds who had gathered outside. There was even a rumour that she was wearing Damart thermal underwear for her visit that day. A beautiful lady who was to be tragically killed in Paris some six years later. Another conspiracy theory arose and is still talked about today.

Life for me was winding down, and we were looking to the future when the children had flown the nest. We loved time together and loved walking in the Dales near Keighley and trips to the beautiful East Coast, Filey, Bridlington and Scarborough, being favourites. Another favourite haunt was the beautiful Spanish island of Majorca. We went as often as we could and would explore the highways and byways of the island, away from the tourist spots and the popular resorts. We loved Majorca so much that it made sense to try and find a base to use on our trips. At the time, property in Majorca and Spain in general was really cheap, the property market was flat. We had a look around and found a one bed apartment which was perfect for our needs. The Majorca climate is fabulous, hardly a cold day ever, although it does rain at times. The locals don't realise what a jewel they have.

A photo I took in Majorca

I could wax lyrical about our times there but now we are in our 80's, we don't get about as much and travelling is very tiring, but if you get chance, have an explore. Even the report of Magalluf is cleaning up its act and its reputation is not as bad as people think.
The pace of life was winding down and I was transferred once again. No fee involved this time. Damart asked me to move from their Head Office in Bingley to the Logistics Warehouse in Steeton and I was to see out my working days there.

Damart is a large mail order company and they send out thousands of parcels every day so we were kept busy. To keep customers sweet they would give people who ordered free gifts. Sometimes the customers kept them and sometimes they were returned, either not wanted or needed. I asked my manager Nancy Farrington what happened to these gifts and she explained they would be disposed of, so being a cheeky Yorkshireman, I asked if I could make use of them for charity. Damart are well renowned for their charity donations and after she had spoken to the top managers, she came back with the good news that I could have a share. So since then to the present day, we have been selling these "free" gifts at church fetes, garden parties etc. and made pots of money for good causes.

Thank you Damart and of course Nancy for helping out. Much appreciated.

CHAPTER 19
1983, A SHINING OF THE LIGHT

Ever since I was born, way back in 1938, I had been brought up to follow the Catholic way of life, my parents being devout Catholics. From my youth, I had always attended mass on Sundays. We attended Our Lady of Victories church in Guardhouse, a region of Keighley.

When I was away from home, I always found a church where I could worship, Loftus Road in London, in Birmingham, Sunderland and in Huddersfield and Peterborough, but in 1983 everything was to change.

Father Michael O'Reilly became the new priest for the Parish and one day at Our Lady of Victories, he took me to one side and said to me, "Why don't you open yourself up to the Holy Spirit? I have seen the blind see, the lame walk and the dumb speak."

Father O'Reilly

To be honest, I thought he was crackers, talking rubbish. It turned out that Father Michael was the spiritual leader of the Charismatic Renewal movement of the Leeds Diocese. I ignored his invitation for weeks, but my wife Brenda started to go to Father Michael's bible study groups and his prayer meetings and one day I decided to go with her and see what it was all about. I wouldn't say I had a "Damascus Road" type experience but it was certainly eye opening and indeed life changing.

All my life I had been a "lukewarm Christian". I used to attend church more to placate my parents and a strict God in heaven. But now the penny had dropped and I realised that God loved me unconditionally.

I made enquiries about the Charismatic Movement:-

It was formed in 1966 by William Storey and Ralph Keifer from Duguesne University in the USA. It was formed to feel the power of the Holy Spirit outside the confines of mass. Their description of the baptism of the Holy Spirit is "A personal experience of the presence and power of the Holy Spirit, who brings alive in new ways the graces of our baptism. The Holy Spirit not only sets on fire all that we have already received but comes again in power to equip us with his gifts for service and mission."

The group of students prayed for months and eventually their prayers were answered and more and more people "saw the light". Now over 100 million Catholics are involved with the movement. This "movement" came to the notice of the Pope fairly early on and he invited those involved to a meeting at the Vatican, where Charles Whitehead had the audacity to tell the Pope to read the Bible, especially "The Acts of the Apostles". The Pope did as he was told and gave his blessing to the movement and the headquarters of the Catholic Charismatic Renewal movement is now at the Vatican.

I started spreading the word and as the representative of Our Lady of Victories, we came together with other faiths to form on interfaith group consisting of Muslims, Buddhists as well as Christians, making worship a great experience for all.

Our group tried to help others both locally and globally. We held garden parties and fetes to help raise money for local causes. On one occasion, Mr Gallagher used to being his pet mice with him to show the local children and provide a talking point. Unfortunately on one occasion, he left them unattended and somebody thought they were vermin after the cakes on display and destroyed them. So off to the pet cemetery, for the undertaker it was a busman's holiday!

When the penny does drop and you realise you are loved unconditionally, it's a new ball game, and it's not cricket or football!

"I am the Way, the Truth and the Life"

"No one can come to the Father except through me." and "Before Abraham was, I am". These verses took on a new meaning. My thoughts went back to a book I had read a few years earlier by a Jesuit priest Anthony Mello, entitled "The Song of the Bird". A story which offers a good illustration of the message of Ezekiel – "Shake off the crimes you have committed and make yourselves a new heart and new spirit".

When he was young, he was a revolutionary and his prayer to God was "Lord give me the energy to change the world". By the time he reached middle age, he realised that half his life had gone and he had not changed a single soul. He changed his prayer to "Lord give me grace to change all those who come in contact with me, my family and friends and I shall be satisfied." By the time he had grown older, his prayer changed to "Lord, give me the grace to change myself." If I had prayed for this right from the start, I should have wasted my life.

Catholic priests seem to move on very quickly, spreading the word and doing good deeds to aid communities. So Father O'Reilly moved on to a city diocese in Leeds and was replaced by Father Michael Powell, who arrived in Keighley with a new set of ideas and plans. He was chaplain at Armley Prison in Leeds and had seen his share of deprivation and poverty in the inner city. He wanted his new flock to help in decreasing poverty, locally and around the world. So he got in touch with the Bishop of Leeds who had connections in Cape Town, South Africa.

Father Michael suggested that our church, Our Lady of Victories, could be twinned with a church in a township near Cape Town. A partnership was set up with St Raphael's Church, based in the township of Kylechia near Cape Town and Father Michael thought it would be a good idea to arrange a visit to see the problems for ourselves.

South Africa in the early 90's was a troubled place. Apartheid had come to an end but trouble was still simmering under the surface. Apartheid was a policy brought in in 1948 by the South African government to segregate the population into groups formed by the colour of their skin. The "white" minority and the "non-white" majority were not allowed to mix together, and racial segregation ran from political to economic discrimination. Non-whites were not allowed to travel, mix or socialise with the white population, and understandably there was a lot of tension and sometimes bloodshed. The non-whites were housed in ghettos known as the "black townships", nothing more than basic materials thrown together, tin huts surrounded by fences.

Father Michael arranged to go to the townships and asked if Brenda and I would accompany him. We jumped at the chance to try and help. We had no idea what to expect, having only seen scenes on TV, as we set off on the long 24 hour journey to South Africa. We arrived at night and under cover of darkness, we were driven to the house of the resident priest at St Raphael's, where exhausted, we went straight to bed.

We awoke the following morning to an amazing site – thousands and thousands of tin shacks huddled together with no electricity and only one standpipe out in the open to supply water. There were thousands of people wandering aimlessly about, the images on TV were nowhere near telling the true story. What an eye opener.

In South Africa wih Father O'Reilly

When we went outside, we were surrounded by the locals, crowding round the strangers from the UK. But in spite of the poverty, everyone had a huge smile on their faces and we were made so welcome. After breakfast, we were invited to look around some of the shacks. Those were the people's houses and they were so proud to show us round. Nobody had anything of any value and the floors were just mud, but the pride of the owners shone out.

All the local churches came together to try to help with the poverty and improve the conditions of the residents of the township. Next door to the church was a school run by the Nuns of Mother Teresa, who also ran an orphanage for the many parentless children. We were invited to share food by the residents. They didn't have enough for themselves but were happy to share with complete strangers. We had come to help them and the roles were now reversed. We were deeply touched by this Christian act, thinking of others before yourself.

The children were so excited to see us and show us their schoolwork. They were lacking in the basics of school equipment and we made lists of all the things they needed. When we returned to the UK, we started to collect the basics to send to South Africa, and we sent things from Our Lady of Victories to St Raphael's for years to come, with the help of Margaret Ward, who was the deputy head of Our Lady of Victories School.

Unfortunately with such deprivation and poverty comes criminality and we were told not to venture out on our own, as because of the colour of our skins we would be easy targets for the gangs who roamed the townships. We saw this at first hand one day when we were travelling by car. We stopped at a crossroads and were instantly surrounded by a gang of youths who wanted our valuables and were armed with bricks and stones. The brave priest confronted them, spoke softly to them and they left empty handed. Phew.

My main thought on our visit to the township was, how so many people with so little could still live their lives with smiles on their faces.

FOOD FOR THOUGHT.

CHAPTER 20
BRENDA PATON

Ever since primary school, Brenda and I have had a bond. We were in the same class and spent lots of time together, playing games in the street with all the other street urchins. I used to watch her playing tennis in the street. I say tennis, it was a rope strung across the street and he and her friend tapping the ball to each other, but to Brenda and her friend, it was Wimbledon on finals day and she was the world champion. Just like me pretending to be Stanley Matthews or Tom Finney, the stars of the day.

We were both very shy, not like the youngsters of today, and we grew closer and closer. Brenda lived in Cartmel Road, just round the corner from my house on Sladen Street. She was one of the "gang" who turned up at whichever street was hosting the games. Word soon got around and children from miles around would turn up for the "Olympics" of skipping, hopscotch, football, cricket, and hide and seek.

Growing up on Sladen Street in the war years was hard. Bomb shelters were dug in the ground just in case the Luftwaffe missed their regular targets. Anderson shelters were placed in people's gardens, those that had a garden, no such luxury on Sladen Street. If a bomb hit anything, that would be the end and the Anderson shelters were more a propaganda thing than an actual safety feature. We kids didn't take any notice of those things. If we had a piece of chalk to mark the hopscotch patterns on the street, that was all we were bothered about, along with shouts of "goal", "how's that" and "relief". The nearest we came to knowing about the war was the Pathe News bulletins at the cinema or the "flicks" as we called it then.

Saturday mornings were great at the cinema, watching the cowboy films and cartoons, nobody had TVs then. In fact Brenda's family were one of the first around to get a TV in the early fifties. Odd families got TVs and it was a usual thing to invite all their friends and neighbours into their house to watch the big events on TV – cup finals, royal weddings and great state occasions were broadcast by the BBC.

Just after the war a tragedy was to befall the Royal Family when King George VI died suddenly on 6th February 1952, thus leaving Britain without a sovereign. His daughter Elizabeth, the heir to the throne, was out of the country and had to return quickly to become our queen, Queen Elizabeth II. So the country was in mourning for the King but about to celebrate a Queen. Everything was relayed to the public by the new medium of television. People who had televisions opened up their homes and invited everyone to watch the Coronation. Every available chair and floor space was taken. The Coronation was a magnificent affair with pomp and circumstance on 2nd June 1953, watched by thousands who lined the streets in London and millions who crowded into living rooms across the country. Street parties were held nationwide and everybody partied.

To mark the ascension to the throne, two men climbed the highest mountain in the world, Mount Everest in the Himalayas, a mountain that had never been conquered before. The 29th May 1953 would be the date that Edmund Hilary and Sherpa Tensing Norgay became famous, and they dedicated the climb to Queen Elizabeth.

Television was the new thing and everybody wanted one. Most people rented them, small black and white images were seen in everyone's living rooms. Colour television was still a long way off and was not to become available until 1967. So cinema was still king and all the cinemas in Keighley were usually full of people crowding in to see the films of the day. Fantasia and the Wizard of Oz captivated the people and Brenda and I started to walk the "yellow brick road" down to the town to watch the "movies".

One film shocked everybody. It was "Rock around the clock" with the American Bill Haley. This film saw the audiences getting out of their seats and dancing in the aisles, which was unheard of! Dancing was for the dance halls.

A certain Mr Francis Albert Sinatra was making his name in the music world as well as the likes of Bing Crosby, Jack Jones and Dean Martin. Music was changing from the Big Band sound and a young man was to change music forever, Elvis Presley. "Elvis the Pelvis" or "the King", as he was named, captivated the young girls. Myself and Brenda were more into jazz than the new pop music and Chet Baker, Dave Brubeck, Stan Getz, and Miles Davis were more our cup of tea. We would listen for hours on the radio, or the wireless as it was then known.

As a lad, I joined the Cubs and progressed to the Scouts and Brenda became a girl guide. When the local cub group were stuck for a leader, Brenda stepped in and became an Akala. She kept the young boys in check. By this time I was playing cricket for Keighley. Brenda would come to watch but hated cricket with a passion. She didn't much like football either, calling it "just a game". Not your typical "WAG". I was playing football for Salts FC and doing quite well, and playing for Huddersfield Town in their academy team. We were typical of teenagers at the time. We took things slowly, very slowly. I hadn't a clue at courting, wooing or romance, but then I was probably hung up on sport! We both left school and I got a job at I and I Craven in Dalton Mills, Keighley as an apprentice colour matcher, and Brenda got a job with the Co-op Insurance in Keighley.

Dalton Mills

I lasted about six months at I and I Craven and moved to Salts Mill in Saltaire, another woollen mill. Saltaire had been built by Titus Salt for his mill and he provided houses for his staff and a small village grew up. It was whilst working at Salts Mill, that I started playing football for Salts FC, and as they say "the rest is history" and I was spotted by the QPR scout.
MUCH LATER

Our world came crashing down a few years ago when my beloved Brenda was diagnosed with the onset of Dementia. Small things like memory loss were creeping in. She is managing to control it with the doctor's help and drugs. She laughs and says at least she has a certificate to say she can't remember things and asks what my excuse is! I am her official carer, it's a bit like the blind leading the blind, but I am learning that even at 81 you can still learn. We have joined various organisations such as the Dementia Society and Sporting Memories, run by our local doctors. We promote dementia awareness at local schools and a friend holds a football tournament for the local schools to highlight the condition.

CHAPTER 21
FAMILY

Myself and Brenda have five children, all different characters, all different personalities.

The boys turned out to be sporting but not as I had hoped, neither liking cricket much, so no "White Rose of Yorkshire".

Laurence, the eldest boy, was into athletics, a keen runner. He has completed the London Marathon twice and the Great North Run three times. He joined the RAF, got married to Steph and they have four daughters. He has coached youngsters in athletics and now travels the world with his job, and is still exploring the countryside, running and walking in his spare time.

He tells the story of the rivalry between Newcastle United and Sunderland, whilst in Newcastle for the Great North Run. He got a taxi from his hotel in Newcastle to Sunderland and the taxi driver would not drive into the town as he was an avid Newcastle fan, and would not be seen dead in Sunderland!! Laurence had to walk the last two miles!

Jane is our second child and was born a "Brummie". In her youth she showed great promise in various sports such as tennis, squash, netball and hockey. She was an avid football fan, supporting Liverpool and her idol was Kenny Dalglish. She married and had a daughter Melissa, who is a nurse and a marathon runner, completing three London Marathons, and made lots of money for charity. Melissa is now married to Tom, an Olympic gold medallist at talking!! And they have a daughter Isabella, a great grandchild for us.

Our third child Anne, is the brains of the family, or so she says!. She became a teacher and whilst at Notre Dame College, she met her future husband Harry, a lad from Liverpool, another Liverpool fan. Anne and Harry have two boys, Harry John and Jacob. Both are big strapping lads. Harry John works in the oil industry and has just got married to Amelia. Jacob was a professional rugby union player, starting at Leeds Carnegie, where he was captain and played for England at various levels, captaining the sides. He then moved to the Premiership playing for Gloucester. He now manages Kowloon Rugby Club in Hong Kong.

Our fourth child Richard is the "black sheep of the family". Brenda says he was a little devil growing up, never doing what he was told and being a total nightmare, but Richard thinks he is the darling. Brenda was rushed back to Yorkshire to give birth to Richard, which was a waste of time, as he was not interested in cricket. He played Rugby League for local teams, Worth Village, Silsden and Keighley. His job is in the medical vocation, being an ultra sonographer nurse. When he gets a bit giddy, Tracy, can soon calm him down. They have a daughter Hollie who is at Cambridge studying to be a doctor. Hollie is a promising hockey player.

Our youngest is Claire and works in education and has a daughter Caitlyn. She is horse mad, maybe a budding Olympian. Unfortunately Claire lives on the "dark side" in Lancashire! They all keep tabs on us on a daily basis.

So we now have a football team and a few subs. And they all support Liverpool. Harry has a season ticket, it must have rubbed off from him.

                              Mike – Brenda

aurence   Jane   Anne   Richard
   | | | |
ebecca   Melissa   Jacob   Holly
Maisie   Tom   Harry
Rosie | John
Alicia |
   | |
Sienna   Isabella

CHAPTER 22
QUESTIONS, QUESTIONS

Even in my 80's I still get letters and phone calls on a weekly basis – autograph hunters, TV stations, and just fans in general, as well as being asked by people in the town. I get asked to open events and give out prizes to schools, rotary clubs, scout groups, and I have been asked many times to give talks. I even have a gym named after me at the Keighley College, an honour indeed.

I was asked to give a talk at Our Lady of Victories School. After talking to the whole school about my career, and playing for England, there was a question and answer session. A young lad asked me if I knew Bobby Charlton. I said "Yes, I know Bobby, in fact I have slept with him." To this answer, the whole school was in uproar and there was much laughter. The head teacher Mr Devlin intervened and asked if I would rephrase my answer. I stuttered a bit and explained that when I was called up to Hendon to train with the England Squad, I "shared a room" with Bobby!! Normal service was resumed. The youngsters of today had put two and two together and come up with five. Youngsters of today!! This was the same session when I washed the dishes with Alf, after the movie. Occasionally I get asked for a selfie, how things have changed.

I am always asked what it was like to play in front of massive crowds; which were my favourite grounds; who were the best players; who were the hard men – the list is endless. I have lost count of the people who said that they have had trials with professional clubs, but preferred to concentrate on being a bus driver, plumber, painter, candlestick maker. I was having a meal recently with a friend when a guy opposite told my friend that he had had trials as a goalkeeper with Bradford City and that Mike Hellawell had recommended him. My friend said "That's odd, this is Mike sat next to me". The guy nearly choked on his lunch. Neither of us had met before – weird eh!

The stadiums now are magnificent. We went to Sunderland for the last game of the season and the pitch looked like it was the first game – immaculate, not a blade of grass out of place. How things have changed. The best stadiums to play at were the obvious choices, Anfield, Highbury, Old Trafford, White Hart Lane, Villa Park, and Hillsborough. The compact grounds had the best atmosphere, Upton Park, Turf moor, the crowd was virtually on top of you. But the one that stands head and shoulders above them all for passion was Roker Park, the Roker Roar was something else. If you can't get up to play in front of these crowds, you shouldn't be in the game. I felt ten feet tall when the fans chanted my name.

I have played with and against some the great footballers of the England game. Johnny Haynes was the best passer of a football I have ever seen. Even on the mud baths we played on, Johnny could ping a pass 40 or 50 yards direct to a teammate. The best goal scorer by a mile was Jimmy Greaves. He had everything and was a natural goal scorer with electric pace over the ground. He didn't like training though, he said he would be knackered after the warm ups they do nowadays.

Then the "holy trinity" from Manchester United, George Best, the best dribbler, Denis Law, the goal poacher and Bobby Charlton who had it wall. He could pass and shoot from distance with both feet.

In the football league, goalkeepers were excellent. Gordon Banks, the top of the tree, but Pat Jennings from Tottenham Hotspur and Northern Ireland, with the biggest hands I have ever seen ran him a close race. Then Alex Stepey from Manchester United, Peter Bonetti from Chelsea and of course my old team mate Ron Springett.

Danny Blanchflower and Bobby Moore, both cultured half backs, strong in the tackle and with a brain long before their time.

I played against Stanley Matthews once. He was well past his best, probably nearing 50, but you could see the class of the man, he could add 5,000 to a gate.

And the hard men. Every team had a "hard man", someone who was there to soften you up with a crunching tackle, some of which were legal and the ball was somewhere in the vicinity. The list is endless: Tony Kaye of Everton; Peter Storey of Arsenal; Nobby Stiles of Manchester United; Ron (Chopper) Harris of Chelsea; Tommy Smith of Liverpool; Dave McKay of Tottenham Hotspur and Norman (bite your legs) Hunter of Leeds United. In fact the whole Leeds United team could look after themselves. Billy Bremner and Johnny Giles were not afraid of anything or anybody.

Every team seemed to be full of Scotsmen who had crossed the border to ply their trade, a tradition that has died out with the Premier League being so popular and players from all over the world turning up for the big money on offer.

At the top of my tree of best and hard players was a player I played against at Millwall, and who became a team mate at Sunderland. Charlie Hurley, the Irish centre half, a colossus of a man who put players on their backsides for fun but who could play a bit as well. Charlie was the "king" of Roker Park. The fans and the players adored him. I can honestly say I never saw Charlie beaten in the air by any opponent. I look at the best centre half of today, Van Dijk from Liverpool, and if he is worth £80 million then Charlie would be priceless, an immovable rock on the pitch and a gentle giant, off it.

I am often asked if a player such as myself would be okay playing today and the answer is simple – the skilful players will play in any era. The modern player is probably fitter and the game is more tactical, but the conditions now are tremendous, like playing football on a carpet, and the tackling is non-existent. The players fall over at the drop of a hat. If we had gone down feigning injury the manager would not select you the following week.

In my day, a hard tackle would be as good as a goal, the crowd would get up for the game. The atmosphere is not quite as good today I think, due to the fans sitting down. Safer though, after various accidents and incidents. I also think the FA Cup is no longer important to the Premier League clubs, and I think it was a big mistake to play semi-finals as well as the final at Wembley. The "occasion" has been taken away.

The semi-finals were played at Hillsborough, Villa Park, Highbury, Old Trafford and now the faithful have to travel to London. Fans seem to take second seat to the TV.

Some of the tackles in my day were X-rated but if a player hit you hard, you hit them back harder. No yellow or red cards back then, so the "man's game" was a man's game. The full backs I faced tried to whack me from the first minute but not many could catch me (not many could) so they resorted to marking me with two men, so if the first didn't get me, the second one would have a go. Bill Shankley of Liverpool was the first manager who tried that. I was playing for Huddersfield Town when the opponents tried to kick me off the pitch. After about six attempts of replacing my kneecaps, I snapped and smacked the winger on the chin, knocking him to the ground. The crowd went wild, they couldn't believe that "mild Mike" had become "Wild Mike"! The player in question, Dave Wagstaff, couldn't believe it either. The referee came over and had a word with me, warned me to be careful, but said he had asked for it, carry on. The modern players take nothing for granted or chance. Their diets are looked after, they warm up, warm down, tactics, tactics and more tactics. They stay overnight in hotels, even when at home, flying to some games. They have doctors, dentists, physiotherapists, nutritionists, and individual trainers. They are wrapped in cotton wool. Our routine, in the 60's, consisted of two hours training per day and sometimes two hours extra in the afternoon. Once we had finished pre-season training, we were deemed to be fit for the season, with a two hour top up. I wince when I see the modern players slide on their knees after scoring a goal. Wait until they get older and the aches and pains start in their knees, ouch!! When I scored I raised my arms up, I must admit, a great thrill to score a goal, but I got as much of a thrill laying a goal on.

At my first club, Queens Park Rangers, the club got me digs near the ground and on match days I would walk to the ground with the fans, getting there about an hour before kick-off. We would have a short talk on the upcoming game, get changed and then the manager would give us instructions for five minutes, then it would be out for a five minute warm up before kick-off. The match would begin and at half time we would come in for a cup of tea or a slice of orange. The smokers in the side would slink into the toilets for a quick drag. After the game ended, no formalities, a quick shower and home for tea.

Away fixtures were similar, but we met at the ground and took a coach to local away games. If the grounds were further away, we would meet at the train station and all catch the train together and again, straight home after the match.

After training in London, I used to go to Acton to the indoor cricket nets and this is where I became acquainted with Mr Humphrey Littleton and his band, who were also cricket mad. Humph was a well-educated man, Eton educated and they all liked to have a net or two. Humph played the trumpet in his band and also the clarinet. I became good friends with them all – Pat Hawes, Wally Fawkes, Jim Bray, Johnny Parker and the Christie brothers. They all thought they were budding cricketers and played in various charity games when not playing in the band. Humphrey Littleton became a household name and appeared on the BBC for years and packed out all the venues whenever he performed.

When I was transferred to Birmingham City, their fixtures were nationwide, but the procedure was very similar. No long warm up before the game and travelling by coach for the local away games, and most of the times we would travel longer distances by coach, we used to stop at the service stations for a meal on the way back from Everton and Liverpool etc. For the longer journeys to Newcastle and London, we travelled by train with a meal on board on the way home. A fleet of taxis would meet us at the railway station to ferry us to the opponent's grounds, no swanky coaches from an overnight stay in a first class hotel. A meal before a game would consist of a small piece of steak with no trimmings, followed by rice pudding, no fancy diet.

It's altogether a different world to the modern players. Nowadays the modern players go abroad to Dubai or Portugal for "warm weather" training. The nearest we got was Blackpool, training on the beach and running in the freezing Irish sea, but we got to stay in the Norbrech Castle hotel for a week.

Don't get me started about modern cricket! I am a total traditionalist when it comes to cricket, with test cricket being the pinnacle of a cricketer's ability. Modern day cricket does nothing for me at all. In my day, cricket was played on uncovered wickets and if you could bat on those wickets, you could bat on anything. I think of the great batsmen of my day and wonder what they would think of the sloggers of today. PBH May, Colin Cowdrey, Ken Barrington, Tom Graveney and the likes, elegant stroke makers who cherished their wicket as if it was gold bullion. If you played across the line, you were pilloried by the coaches, never mind swiping a ball to "cow corner".

20-20 was a pub game in my day, played after work, but the modern crowds want instant results. There's no patience, just an excuse for a booze up with fancy dress.

Test cricket is dying a death, except for the Ashes which still seems to get the public excited. I can't remember the last time I saw a test match last 5 days unless weather interrupted, all down to the ability of modern day batsmen and their inability to bat for long periods. A quick 40 or 50 seems to be the order of the day, the days of the big 100's are dwindling.

The exceptions to this feeling are the Indian captain Virat Kohli, a class batsman and Steve Smith of Australia. These two value their wicket. The art of proper batting has long gone, most just want to hit sixes. Now the powers that be have introduced a new competition, "the 100" which leaves me cold, another nail in the coffin of cricket. But then again, the TV companies and the money counts and the public will watch in full fancy dress, boozed up.

And to think I rushed Brenda back to Yorkshire for the birth of both our sons so they could play cricket for the county of their birth.

After the huge snowfall of 1947, the next harsh winter was 1963. The frost was horrendous, and for three months the whole structure of the country came to a standstill. The rivers froze over, the snow was not as bad as 1947, but the frost went really deep into the ground, causing multiple cancellations of matches, for weeks on end. A couple of years ago, I was asked by a TV company to give an interview for the "Inside Out" programme for BBC Midlands with regard to the winter of 1963. The modern viewers couldn't get into their heads why the games were cancelled. The winter of 1963 was one of the coldest on record.

I was sad to see the demise of Notts County. They lost their league standing this year and are no longer the oldest league club in the world. That honour now belongs to their local rivals Nottingham Forest.

I was selected for an England XI to celebrate the centenary of Notts County on 27th May 1962. Notts County are famous for lending their kit to a famous Italian side, thus Juventus playing to this day in the black and white stripes of Notts County.

Recently I had a visit from a young lady from the Football Association and the Players' Union. They were checking on the health of ex-players in view of the Jeff Astle enquiry into dementia in footballers who headed the heavy ball in the 60's. I informed her that I skulked on the wing and the only time I headed the ball was when Bill Brown, the Tottenham Hotspur goalkeeper dropped it on my head and it went in for a goal, my only headed goal, in fact my only header. A fluke.

She had travelled from Brentwood in Essex, a bit of a trail for a southern lass who had come up for the day seeing lots of ex-professionals.

CHAPTER 23
PROLOGUE

We still live in Keighley. As Dorothy in the Wizard of Oz says "There's no place like home."

We try to be as active as we can and will soon be celebrating our Diamond Wedding Anniversary. I have 59 medals for good conduct and can't wait til I get the 60th. Brenda is laughing!

Keighley has everything we need. It's on the edge of the beautiful Yorkshire Dales and close to Bronte Country. Haworth is only a couple of miles away. Cliffe Castle and East Riddlesden Hall are on the doorstep and the Lakes are only an hour away.

We have a good circle of friends in the town and we attend bible studies and prayer meetings at All Nations Church, a short stroll from home. We attend meetings at Sporting Memories and Dementia UK.

We keep in touch with Birmingham City and Sunderland and try to attend matches when possible. We have a reunion at Birmingham for the ex-players, especially the League Cup winning team, although we are dwindling now. Sport has been with me all my life and I have made many friendships and many friends that have lasted a lifetime. Through football, I have travelled the world, met royalty and prime ministers. Harold Wilson was an avid Huddersfield Town fan and whenever we were playing in London, he always came into the dressing room to pass on his best wishes. I met another Prime Minister, Edward Heath when we played an exhibition game in Dusseldorf, Germany. Mr Heath was there on a trade mission.

I have played with and against football royalty. But in Brenda's words "It's just a game."

If you have taken the trouble to read my story, thank you, may God bless you and for that matter, if you haven't read it, God bless you too.

I want to say a very special thank you to Father Michael O'Reilly for when he said "The Holy Spirit will teach you everything". He was right and it changed my life forever.

If you have never been to Keighley, please call and see us in "God's Own County".

When I was young, I was told many times that I would never make the grade, as I was too frail, not strong enough. I was rejected by Huddersfield Town and I want to tell everybody "THE IMPOSSIBLE **IS** POSSIBLE".

325 appearances in the Football League, a League Cup Winners medal, Runners up and scorer in the Inter Cities Cup Final, and playing for England twice. Not bad for a "ginger top". Nothing is impossible if you keep trying.

Thank you for reading my story and if we haven't met in this life, see you all in Heaven.

Bless you,

Michael

All Nations church (top left) Dementia friends (top right), our current home (bottom)

Brenda and I on holiday